Olive

A CHILD IN BURMA

Much love — and
thanks for your
friendship —

Grace R.

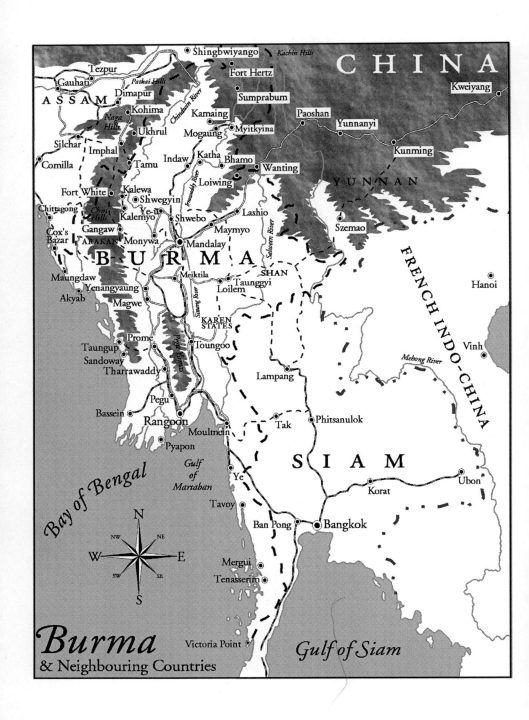

Burma
& Neighbouring Countries

A Child in Burma

By Grace Rorke

First published in 2002 on behalf of the author
by Scotforth Books,
Carnegie House,
Chatsworth Road,
Lancaster LA1 4SL,
England
Tel: +44(0)1524 840111
Fax: +44(0)1524 840222
email: carnegie@provider.co.uk
Publishing and book sales: www.carnegiepub.co.uk
Book production: www.wooof.net

British Library Cataloguing-in-Publication data
A catalogue record for this book is available from the British Library

ISBN 1-904244-15-7

Typeset by Carnegie Publishing

Printed and bound in the UK by Alden Digital, Oxford

For Alan and Tucker

We Three were as one, though one has gone,
the bond has never been broken

We shall meet again

Contents

Illustrations

Foreword

THIS IS A BOOK about a magic childhood. Early on, Grace Rorke writes of it as: *our own world of adventure, of secrets and the future so far ahead that we had no wish to be grown up.* 'We' are Grace or 'Gracie' and her two adored brothers, Alan and Tucker – there are older sisters, but they are not part of the conspiracy. Imagine a world both exotic and familiar; a world of big safe gardens; of ravishing smells and succulent fruits, of trees to climb and water to splash in; of – on the whole – approving if firm parents; of pets both wild and tame; of gangs without violence and school playgrounds without bullying, all in the peaceful and harmonious setting of pre Second World War Burma and you have the frame and scale of this delightful memoir.

E. Nesbit meets Enid Blyton with a touch of Rumer Godden. Reading *A Child in Burma* I couldn't help thinking, a little wistfully, of the freedom children once enjoyed to 'play' – playfulness being, in my opinion, the main hope of childhood and the most important gift of living. Grace Rorke has a wonderful eye and ear for playfulness: for her wonderfully wise grandmother, for the eccentric chutney-making Mr Walker, for their ebullient railway-king Uncle Tom, for the water fights in the bathroom and, during the water-festival, in the street, for the joys and dangers of kite flying, for the sound of a friendly tiger rubbing its back against the sides of their hill-bungalow, for the common-sense and tenderness of the local Japanese doctor, Dr Suzuki.

She notes, too, the darker side of things: the wornout legs of the rickshaw pullers, the diseases that could strike without warning, the riots that nearly killed her father, the danger of bandits and above all the invasion of Japan in 1942 that ended her Burmese childhood and changed the history of Asia.

But this is a child's-eye view and therefore fundamentally optimistic, seeing the light and the comedy even at the darkest and potentially most tragic times. As Gracie, Alan and Tucker say farewell to 'My Own Self's House', the most loved of their Burmese homes, before setting out on their long journey of escape from the advancing Japanese, they know that they will never come back and that life will never be the same again but that equally nothing can take away those enchanted Burmese days and a childhood they can build on forever.

A tale to treasure.

Piers Plowright
June 2002

Note Bene: Piers Plowright was a BBC Radio Drama producer between 1967 and 1997. He has lived in the Far East and has worked with Grace Rorke in Radio Drama Productions.

Prologue

W HY WRITE THIS BOOK? So many people can go back to the places where they were born – retrace their steps and walk along paths they trod as young children. They see changes through the years, but certain places always remain – the streets, even the skyline. But for many like myself there is no going back, for war and circumstance have obliterated the places we once knew, and so we have only our cherished memories.

Burma was a beautiful country. A country of gentle, kind and welcoming people as a nation. No country throughout history is without its faults or corruption and greed, much of which has led to the problems Burma and so many nations face today. But as a child and until the invasion of Burma by the Japanese, Burma was a land of beauty, freedom, light and a funny word to use in this day and age, of safety. No matter what took place there was this over-riding feeling of being safe. As children we roamed wherever we wanted without fear. And our friends were Burmese and Indians, and before the war, Japanese and Chinese. What a wonderful mixture of nationalities and we all got on with each other. The Karens, further North where we went on holidays, are a lovely tribe. What else can I say? The Gold Mohor tree, or the Flame of the Forest as it is commonly known, with its small green leaves and beautiful red flowers and near white bark which lined avenues and lit up the sky, and which transformed any garden into paradise. The flowers, the variety of fruit, all, all was a part of a country that embraced all peoples. A land of pagodas and exotic dress and beautiful women – a land that is today so yearningly in my memories and is no more. The land is there, the people are there, but the freedom and safety are gone. But my thoughts, my memories linger – and I still dream on.

CHAPTER ONE

Grandma's House

'We're going to visit Grandma.'

M Y NAME IS GRACE. Gracie to my family and friends. That Mother often called me dis-Grace was no reflection on her, but rather on myself, for I was a very independent soul.

When I was born – in the Dufferin Hospital in Rangoon, Burma – I came so fast that I nearly ended up in the toilet which Mother was visiting at the time. No wonder I looked disgruntled and had an anxious frown on my face, which caused the doctor to remark to my Mother, 'You're going to have trouble with this one.' My Mother often reminded me of this during one of our little arguments. I always lost, which was as it should be. Little children should never argue with parents who know best. Whether it is the best for the child or the parent at that time in my life I never worked out!

Rangoon – Burma. Myanma it is now called but I still only think of it as Burma, for as a child that was home to me. I look back on my childhood with a sense of awe and wonderment. Family problems and fortunes by-passed me. I know now that things were not always good, but for me and my two brothers in those early years life was a constant source of discovery and a 'what's next' and 'what do you think is round-the-corner' existence, especially at Grandma's house.

The excitement, the leaping of the heart, the knot of expectation those words brought, 'We're going to visit Grandma', were as nothing compared to the deep joy and peace it brought to my fast beating heart. I never asked my brothers if they felt as I did. Maybe it was because their shining faces said it all.

My two brothers! Thomas and Alan – but Tucker and Allo to me – were an extension of myself. Fifteen months between the boys and seventeen months between Tucker the middle one and myself the youngest. Alan was the one who was the anchor man. The steady, reasonable peace maker who rarely got into trouble. Tucker was the wild cannon who had the grin of an angel and who could talk himself out of any situation, and with his charm got away with just about everything. Which left me! I was always in trouble, because I couldn't talk my way out of anything. I've never been a good liar, but somehow always managed to look guilty even when I was not. So when I said, 'I didn't,' no one believed me.

Grandma's House

She had come to Burma in the late 1800s when my father was a year old. Grandfather had been in the British Colonial Army and died of a heart attack and is buried in Bedford, England. He had talked of Burma, so Grandma, with her Mother (my Great-Grandmother whose husband had died in the Indian Mutiny) decided to go to Burma. Quite a courageous step to take with four young children. But one she never regretted – nor did we, for we had a childhood that was full of adventure of one kind or another. She bought land outside Rangoon at a place called Insein, and built a house.

A house like no other house – looked like no other house and with an atmosphere that even today I could not describe. The land was virtually in jungle, which had to be pushed back. Through the years it was pushed even further back as other families moved in and Insein became a small settlement in its own right. But when Grandma built things were pretty tough. I think – or I like to think – that Grandma had children in mind when she built the house. Certainly she had four of her own when she had it built 15 feet off the ground, on one foot square

pillars which went deep into the ground. It was very practical
what with snakes and the odd wild animal around. The Burmese
also, especially near water, built their homes on stilts too. Not
in the towns, but mainly in the villages.

The base of the house was made of very hard baked earth. I
suppose it had a mixture of stone, cement etc to withstand the
torrential rains, but I am only remembering what it was to me
as a child. But the wooden posts must have gone very deep for
the house stood as firm as a rock. The base itself was raised
and on a higher level than the land around, although it could
not have been too high for I could always leap up, even as a
tiny tot. The roof was of corrugated tin. I was told it started off
with a thatched roof, but too many small animals and birds
made their home in the thatch so it was prudent to change it.
But when the monsoons – the rainy season came – wow! The
noise was deafening and rather scary – but at night it was
exciting. And when there was thunder and lightning, which was
often, it was awesome. The trees surrounding the house were
vast bamboo, banyan, jackfruit and mango trees among others,
and the swish and whistle of the bamboo as the wind tore
through the trees sent shivers up my spine. As Grandma had
never wanted electricity we only had candles and lamplight. I
can still conjure up the feeling I had then. Of feeling totally
isolated in a world of crashing thunder and wind and rain –
rain hitting the roof like someone pouring cascades of stones
down on us – a world where no-one else existed. Lightning
lighting up the trees, which in the darkness suddenly appeared
like monstrous giants, swaying in the wind – oh, how wondrous
are the elements and how frightening they can be. But I was
never afraid, and even now the elements do not frighten me,
though I do respect what they can do and would never take
chances. But as a child in Grandma's house there was such a
sense of security. No harm, I knew, would come to us in Her
House!

She had also cultivated an area she had fenced off, in front
of the house. This was her garden and was her pride and joy:
Grandma's Garden. I remember roses, cannas with their bright

yellow and red flowers, phlox with their wonderful fragrance, and other flowers the names of which I do not remember. It was a place of quiet and beauty and colour. It had a gate at the far end which led onto a green hill which sloped gently down to the family well.

That 'green hill'. What did it mean to me? It was really only a big mound which was surrounded by trees – but it was my place. It seemed apart from the rest of the land which was vast and which we roamed at will – but my green hill? Somehow I was the only one who came there and I still don't know why, but it was always my place. I've never shared this with anyone before, not even my beloved brothers. It was my green hill of hopes and dreams. I wanted to act and I've never desired to do anything else – but as dreams went they were vivid and wonderful. I knew the dreams, then, were but dreams. What did I from such an early age know of the world of the theatre or the outside world? It wasn't something that the family indulged in, yet inside of me were other characters bursting to come out. And so they did on my green hill. I made up situations, I acted each character in turn, and the fact that today I have put so much of that into practice should give hope to all who dream. And what about hope? Would anything come of my dreaming? I know that the two were always bound up with each other. Easy to dream, and at four years of age could I dare to hope? The only film I had seen was *The Blue Bird* starring Shirley Temple. And who was I, who did I know? Who knew what was going on inside of me? My brothers did know up to a point, but oh the yearning, the longing, the wanting so much! I escaped from the world on my green hill.

I talked to God too. He too was part of my life and at times Jesus was the only friend I had, certainly when my brothers and I were parted at a later date ... I've always chattered to Him, but in those days it wasn't something that would have gone down too well. God was up in heaven and awesome. That

I found Him very accessible would have been hard to explain to grown-ups who knew it all. But on my green hill, all, all was possible. Acting my heart out, singing my heart out – my heart would soar to limitless heights, I would feel free and alive. I have only to close my eyes to feel the softness of the grass under my feet, for I like to run barefoot.

I always thought I was not observed from the house, but Grandma told me many years later that she had often seen me and wondered if perhaps one day all the dreams I acted out would come true. She prayed that they would. Looking back I realize that my Grandma was the only grown-up who truly understood me. The real me! The only one who understood what was going on in my heart. For although I was a very independent child, that very independence was born of a fear of anyone finding out my innermost thoughts and feelings for who would understand my dreams? It would have been a terrible thing to be laughed at for my dreams, and also because I thought myself to be rather plain and skinny with straight golden hair. I so longed for Mother to let me grow it, but that was never to be. So apart from my brothers I tried not to depend on anyone and kept my innermost thoughts to myself. I really did think I was so very plain and for countless years believed this to be so. And it all happened because of a situation the family – the grown-ups – did not explain to me.

A cousin was getting married and I so hoped to be a flower girl. Oh how I wanted it; a pretty dress and a circlet of flowers in my hair. I waited and waited to be asked. Surely they wouldn't leave me out? But they didn't and asked a little girl my age instead who wasn't even in the family. I thought my heart would break, but I wasn't going to let anyone see it. Even when this same little girl told me it was because she was pretty and had dark curly hair. Oh the pain of it! I remember asking God to give me curly hair, so I too could be chosen. But it was not to be, and we all went to the wedding and I had to watch, my little heart bursting with pain and humiliation. It was when I was much older that I was told it was because the family disapproved of the marriage, which turned out to be a very good one. But to a little girl who hadn't been told, I lived with the surety that it was because I was plain and always would be. Dear grown-ups! There are some things kids need to know. Otherwise their imaginations can lead to all kinds of things. In my case to a lot of inner pain.

So that's my green hill for you. It is no more, for when the Japanese invaded, Insein, being near the airport, was heavily bombed and the whole area flattened. Not a tree or bush remained. When father returned after the war, the only way he knew where the house had once stood was because he found the well. As Grandma and my Aunt had had to leave everything behind except for some clothes and a few small treasured possessions, it was terrible for father.

But back to the house! It was made of a variety of woods. Oblong in shape, it had a centre room which stretched the length of the house and off this room on either side were two large bedrooms, a box room and a bathroom. Running the length of the house off the bedrooms were verandas. The bathrooms were on a lower level – five steps down, for I counted them every time (don't ask me why) when I used the bathroom. The kitchen was a separate building from the house, as was often the case in homes such as these. Very often they were also living quarters for the cook and *Ayah*. In this case our *Ayah* was the cook and very much a member of the family. All our servants were. People often say, 'Oh, you had servants did you?', and make it sound bad. But for people like my Grandma and my family having a cook or a *chokra*, which is a lad who does all kinds of things, and a *mali* – who is a gardener – and of course an *Ayah* who helps with the kids, is no different than having a charlady here, or a gardener or a nanny. Except that we as a family treated them as family, and I should know. Many were the times that my *Ayah* spanked my bottom with Mothers say-so if she wasn't there. The cooking was done on a coal or wood stove as there was no electricity to Grandma's house. But in the dining

Grandma's House

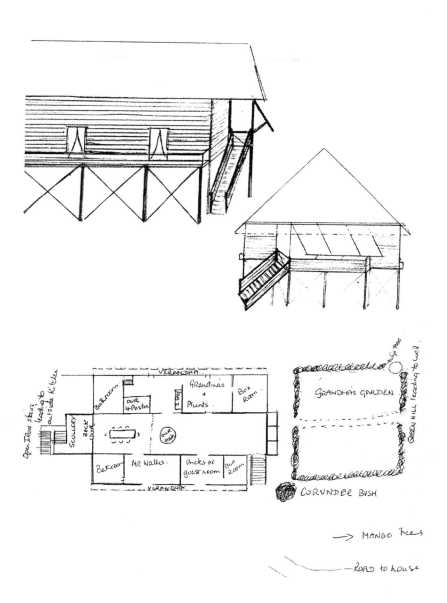

Grandma's House at Insein.

section of the house there was a two-burner oil stove over which the milk was boiled each night. But the most unusual feature of the house was the lack of a front door.

The stairs leading into the house were what today would be called open-plan. But these were open in more ways than one. They came up on the outside of the left half of the front of the house, looking at the house from the front. At the top of the stairs was a slatted gate leading into the front section of the middle room. All one had to do was put out your hand over the top and lift the latch. We kids used to stick our fingers through. It was ironic that the house had a back door with a huge bar across it, and you will think us a queer lot when I tell you that no one could go to sleep until the back door was bolted and barred. My Great-Grandmother, Granny to us, I remember saying 'Better to see the enemy coming then have him strike from behind'. The reason I remember these words is because Grandma often recalled them in the years ahead.

But regardless of these precautions we did have the odd intruder, both human and animal. Before I was born there was an occasion when a bear came to visit. I believe it was someone's pet which had broken free. The *Ayah* at that time was sweeping the house and Mr Walker, who lived with the family, and I can't ever remember him not being around, was pottering around in his room, when *Ayah* heard a scratching at the back door and took no notice. But when she heard sounds at the front gate she went to investigate, and there was the bear. One would have expected a scream and hysterics but not our tiny but valiant *Ayah*. Yelling for Mr Walker, who came running, she walloped the bear on its nose and between the two of them gave that bear the worst time of its life. It retired in disgust, never to return again.

On another occasion when Mr Walker had reason to be away on business for a few days, after Grandma had awakened to find a dark face peering down on her through the mosquito net – Granny had decided to take a few precautions. This consisted of placing a basin of water at each doorway. At about 2 a.m. everyone was awakened by yells and screams and the odd curse, only to find Granny with an upturned basin near her and soaking wet. She had completely forgotten the basins she had placed there. After this episode it was decided that the safety of the family was best left in the hands of the Almighty.

Another facet of this unique and wonderful house was the front. I'll try to explain. The front section of the centre room, which as I said earlier ran the length of the house, was the sitting room, or drawing room or living room or whatever people like to call it. But I do know it was where visitors were entertained – but I will come to more explanations later. Where the steps leading into this area were open, so too was the front part of the house. With a difference. In most cases there would have been a wall and windows. But here the wall was only about three feet high, the rest of the 'wall' consisted of three huge flaps which hung from under the roof of the house on hinges. These flaps could then be pushed outwards and upwards by long poles which hooked on the wall. So the whole front of the house could be opened up, by one or by all three shutters, depending on the weather. A marvellous way of air-conditioning, and on a hot day the air just flowed through.

The wall met the small section into which the gate fitted. Added to this were the floorboards. These were about three to four inches wide and made of whitish wood. No idea what, and as I write this there is no one to ask, but it is not too important. But what is, is the fact that there was a gap between each floorboard giving more airflow – for none of the bedrooms had windows. It was very inconvenient for us kids, because on a rainy day the grown-ups could see what we were up to underneath the house.

As a child I had a terrible fear of going blind. I don't quite know why, but I think it started the first time I was on my own at Grandma's house without my brothers. I was very small at the time. As I said, there were no windows and as the walls of the house were made of overlapping lengths of wood, no light penetrated. Not that it would have made much difference if there had been cracks, for we were surrounded by trees, with no electricity therefore no street lighting. Total blackness. With my brothers I could just curl up and sleep, but alone was another matter. I'd try to sleep, hoping I'd fall asleep before the grown-ups went to bed and all the lamps were put out, but I was so afraid I never did. The blackness was so complete that if I closed my eyes tight I could see patterns behind my eyes – perhaps an expert can explain that – and when I opened them, blackness! And that was when I thought I would never see again. Terrified of never seeing again, I would fall asleep, exhausted of course, but that was no consolation, even though it was an enormous relief to find I could see the next morning. Till the next night! My Aunt wouldn't let me have a little light and said 'Don't be silly', but my lovely Grandma, seeing the dark circles under my eyes asked me if all was well. So I told her I was afraid of the darkness. I never told her of my fears of never seeing again. So she gave me a little torch and said, 'We won't tell anyone else, just keep it under your pillow and when the darkness is too much, just switch it on.' So the fear that haunted me slowly faded, for that little torch went on and off till I was finally reassured. Oh, the fears little children have! Fears all too real in a little child's mind. Rationality doesn't enter into it. I always have a light burning when my grand-children visit.

The approach to the house was by a long winding road. Other houses had been built here and there through the years, though none like Grandma's. Hers was the first and as the jungle had been cut back, so the road to the house was like no other road either. I called it the 'sea-sand road', because it was made of deep white sand – from whence it came I do not know. It was never tarmacked. Always difficult to walk on and hard for cars in the rainy season, it was a nightmare for the rickshaw man. The narrow wheels of the rickshaw would get imbedded in the sand and the poor chap just couldn't pull it out, especially with

Burmese rickshaw

HOOD TO BE PULLED OVER
WHEN NEEDED.

passengers. On one occasion, the rickshaw carrying Grandma
and my Aunt upended in a rut and they were tipped backwards.
Following this rather unpleasant incident it was decided that at
a particular point all passengers would be unloaded and walk
the rest of the way. Hard to tell who was the most upset, the
rickshaw man faced with his passengers on their backs, their
legs in the air and their skirts around their waists, or Grandma
and my Aunt, who being rescued and their dignity restored
vowed never to go in a rickshaw again. Of course they did. But

my Grandma, who used to tell us kids all these stories, always laughed when she recalled this particular incident. I loved my Grandma, she was an inspiration to me then, and even today I get a warm feeling just remembering her.

But it was a lovely road and a lovely walk. Mango trees formed a belt to one side, the tall trees with their branches overlapping and spreading out. Wonderful, especially when the fruit ripened and the time came for picking – and eating! A delicious time indeed! The sea-sand road gradually became harder as it neared the house, pebbles now mixed with the sand. We children loved walking down this road shoeless. I need no excuse to do without shoes; even today I discard them when I can. The result: healthy, corn-free feet. So my brothers and myself used to pick up the pebbles with our toes and see who could throw them the furthest. By the time the road came to the area surrounding the house the ground was rock solid.

To the right of the stairs leading into the house stood a large prickly bush with hard red and white berries. It was called a corrunder bush. I've never heard of one since nor set eyes on one. But that was what it was called. The fruit was inedible, though it looked good. It was good to sit under too on the odd occasion. I have a picture around somewhere of my father and his two brothers taken near it; one of the few pictures remaining of our time there as we lost so much when the Japanese invaded.

Of the main household who lived in Grandma's house there was my Aunt and Mr Walker and my father's middle brother. And of course Granny, who died when I was five years old going on six. There was another Aunt but she was bedridden and had something wrong with her spine. I cannot remember what she looked like for we seldom saw her, but I remember her cries, 'Oh my back, my back'. I wished I could just touch her and make her better, but I guess little girls didn't do things like that, even though I knew the bible stories about the things Jesus did and I didn't see why he didn't do it now – but that was then. So I would run away and cry for her. My memory of her is of her pain, and my wish that she could be well again.

The Aunt who was left never married. She was a school teacher and worked as a private tutor. She was very beautiful and had many suitors but nothing came of any of them, which was sad. I was too young to understand all these things, but I did wonder if her sharp tongue frightened them off the way it did me. I got to know her better in later years, but I still had reservations in that direction.

My Granny was a dear. Tall, very straight-backed – very regal. She had snow-white hair which fell well below her waist (why couldn't I have long hair also?), which she coiled round and round her head. I was the cause of her losing a clump of that gorgeous hair, and I bore the disgrace of that for many years. Today it is a memory I can talk about and laugh over, but the reality at that time was very different. It happened like this. Granny loved having her hair combed, and on this day she asked if I would like to comb it. I can't have been more than five years old and had to stand on a stool. I remember the comb was white and about five inches long. All went well for a while and it was lovely combing that white silvery silky hair. Then I made a fatal mistake. I took the comb to the very edge of the hair and began to roll a section of the hair round the comb. Round and round I went till I got to the nape of her neck. Alas I couldn't unravel it, it was firmly knotted in the teeth of the comb. I tugged and pulled and things got worse. My hands got hot and sticky, my knees began to feel weak and my heart was thumping with fear. Granny began to suspect something was wrong, and said, 'Gracie dear why are you tugging so?', in her sweet soft voice. I could barely answer when my brother Alan came in, took one look at what was happening and made a hurried exit. I didn't blame him, this was my mess. By this time my legs were like jelly, I was so scared that I didn't think I would survive the next few moments of my life. I was about to tell Granny what I had done when the worst possible person to come in appeared – my Aunt! With her I didn't stand a chance. I knew I was going to die. She took one look and hit

Ellen 'Granny' (author's great-grandmother).

the ceiling, or rather the rafters for we didn't have a ceiling. She convinced Granny, she certainly convinced me, that all Granny's beautiful hair had to be cut off. I was also the naughtiest child – I would have said the unluckiest – child alive and I deserved a good spanking which she proceeded to put into practice there and then. Granny came out of her first shock and said, 'Stop that at once and hand me a mirror'. She then took the mirror and a pair of scissors, surveyed the damage and began to cut very carefully. That done, she coiled the rest of her abundant hair round her head into her 'granny's knot' and that was that. She then took the comb with her hair wrapped round it and said with a twinkle in her eyes, 'Well I have enough hair thank God to hide this, but I think we will keep this as a souvenir, eh Gracie?' And kept it was, by all the wrong people who reminded me every so often of my wickedness and the day I ruined my Grandmother's hair. My Aunt thought I had been let off too lightly and found other ways of making me pay for it. At that young age it was very hard. No one ever knew how close I was to actually collapsing with terror; I could hardly breathe and was sure I would die. Actually at that moment I would not have minded – it would have been preferable.

Mr Walker on the other hand was a friend to us children, and made up for a lot of hassle from my Aunt. I think everyone knew the situation and came down on the side of us kids, which was a blessing. He also liked his hair played with, but in a different way. He told us he had a blue mole on his head, which moved around, and we needed to find it. So we agreed to hunt for it, and whichever one of us was available at the time a-hunting we would go. He would sit in his cane lounger and off we would go. We would start in one spot and he would say, 'I think its moved here, it's itching'. Bless him! We realized it was all a put up job for he had very little hair, but we knew he liked his head scratched and little fingers playing softly in what hair he had, so we didn't mind. It was never for long anyway as the sensation sent him to sleep and we would creep away. Many years later when he was a very old man and still in Burma – he remained there during the Japanese occupation

– I wrote to him reminding him of his blue mole, and I have a letter from him tucked away. The other lovely thing he used to do was make delicious pickles and chutneys. These he used to make underneath the house. He had an old fashioned stove in which he heated his jars and sterilized them. I can use these words now, but then I only vaguely understood why he did it. He also had an open fire with a grid over which he stirred his mixtures. Then, after he had filled his jars, he used a cork as a lid and then sealed it with sealing wax. Or something very like. But I used to watch enthralled as he melted the wax and poured it over the cork, sealing the jar. Oh the wonderful odours that wafted up through the floorboards! Mango, lime, bringal (aubergine) pickle and mango and tomato chutney. And even Balachoung, a Burmese delicacy made from dried prawns and other ingredients. As I write the very thought of it makes my saliva glands work. To the uninitiated Balachoung smells of the worst kind of rotting matter while it's cooking. But once ready! Pure delight. When Mr Walker had one of his cooking sessions, all else stopped. The peeling of onions, the cutting up of garlic, the grinding and pounding of all the ingredients – for everything was fresh, nothing came from a packet – and the red and green chilies which made eyes smart and noses itch. It was a delightful time for my brothers and I. It would be some time before we tasted of these delights, but Mr Walker liked his products to 'rest', so we had to be patient. As there were so many other things to do that time soon passed. Dear, dear Mr Walker.

My Father was the youngest of four. My Aunt was the eldest and Dad the youngest. His middle brother also lived in Insein. He had a daughter slightly younger than myself, an only child, and I think she went to boarding school, or somewhere similar because we only ever saw her occasionally. She used to get me into terrible trouble for some reason. I liked her for she was such a generous child. But if she did something wrong she always said that I had done it, and as my Aunt was the one who looked after her, and she also had a cherubic smile like Tucker, I was never believed. Oh dear. She would follow me around and do everything I did and repeat everything I said. I would say, 'Don't do that' and she would say, 'Don't do that'. This would go on for days and then I would finally get angry and she would say she hadn't done anything, so Gracie once more was in the doghouse. My Mother realized this and so it was seldom that I was there at the same time. My dear Grandma didn't notice and I wasn't going to tell tales. But things were better as we grew older and a lot wiser, especially as I began to learn very fast that if my brothers were not around there was only myself to stand up for myself. And I did. But that was later. It never happened to me when Mr Walker was around for he was always my champion.

Grandma and my Aunt were a bit old-fashioned when it came to dresses. They always had to be well below the knees. My cousin's dresses were all like that. Mine were not, but the hems were always put down on my dresses when I went to Grandma's, and promptly put up again by Mother when I got home again. It was an indignity I put up with, but out of sight I soon tucked my dress into my knickers and got on with climbing trees and being whatever character I had decided to be that day.

My Grandma and Granny didn't believe in single beds, though I think there was one. So each of the four bedrooms had double beds and one even had two. The rooms were large so there was enough space. All were four-posters and had mosquito nets. The one Allo, Tucker and I had was in the right back bedroom and was huge. Vast to us little things! Everything looks bigger when you are small. Our bed stood well off the floor and had a deep feather mattress and two wonderful bolsters. The bolsters were a joy to our young hearts and made going to bed an adventure. For these bolsters were often an aeroplane which Alan flew, as he wanted to be a pilot when he grew up – which he did become.

Tucker wanted to be a racing driver, which he didn't become, and so each night there were all the sounds of cars revving and planes taking off. I was always the passenger and happy to be so, and when we had a collision I was the nurse. Never any trouble being sent to bed, for I recall bedtime being an extension

Jeanne Rorke (author's grandmother).

of play-time. While they had their dreams and acted them out in the big bed, I had my 'green hill'. Finally we would curl up and sleep contentedly. Tomorrow we knew would be as good as today.

The run-up to bedtime was a very cosy time. Earlier I said that the front section of the big middle room was for visitors. The layout is important, so you can imagine what it was like. It was divided into three parts. The first had Granny's rocking chair and two lounging cane chairs with wooden arms. These had two extra arms which you were able to swivel out and use as leg rests. Then there were the *Morras*, which were cane stools about two feet high. The top and bottom were round and the same size, but the middle tapered to a waist ... then there was a card table, a beautiful side table and a centre table. Then came the next section which I always called ours. For here at a big round table we spent the evenings. Nearby stood an easel, much higher than I was and on which stood a picture of Granny's husband. It was an enlarged portrait taken from an original drawing by Great-Grandmother on Great-Grandfather's side. It was so real that I used to have long conversations with him. There is a long story attached to this picture but not relevant to our childhood. After this part where our round table stood, there were two large partitions with a wide opening in the centre which sectioned off the living area from the dining room. No ceiling, just rafters and huge cross-beams on which rested the roof. The lamplight just dissolved into the darkness and we were cocooned in a cosy circle of lamplight. The darkness reared up and away, never harming us, where small lizards and spiders happily went about their lives.

But round our table all was safe and secure. We would read or play cards, draw, do jigsaws or build card houses. A favourite pastime for us, for we would put all the packs together and build and build till the table was covered and no one dared breathe until it was finished. Then we all puffed and the whole lot would come tumbling down! We would also play snap and beggar my neighbour and get very excited. Tucker always won and I'm sure he cheated, though I never knew how; but I never won. Alan did at times, but I think he was on to Tucker's wiles. Tucker always won any argument and we always said later that he should be a Counsel for the Defence in a court of law, for he would always get his clients off no matter what the crime. He certainly won all our games! I love my brother dearly, but his mischievous grin disarmed all but the toughest, and they always caved in finally.

At the end of the evening came family prayers. We all enjoyed them. Tucker was very funny. When Mother was teaching us the names of the twelve disciples, Simon the Canaanite was one of them. Tucker misheard and for years thought that Simon became a Knight. We knew and loved all the Bible stories from the Old and New Testaments. We reckoned that the Bible had every adventure that there ever was in it. After family prayers, we had a hot drink. Horlicks! Grandma would heat the milk up on the stove and then make the Horlicks. I wonder if today there is the same contraption she had. It looked like a long thick oblong glass vase and it had a steel plunger. She would put the Horlicks and the milk in and then use the plunger. Up and down – squish! squish! squish! – until it was mixed and all frothy. Poured the Horlicks into tumblers for us and we'd sip it happily. Delicious! Horlicks has never tasted again like it did then.

Then there was the 'tucktoo.' Grandma had two shelves built in our section standing high off the floor, on angled brackets. She kept her special bits of china on these. Resting on the brackets were trays under each shelf. And behind one of these the tucktoo made his home. He was a lizard about nine inches long and we called him the tucktoo because that was the sound he made. He had lived behind that tray for as long as we could remember and as no one wanted to disturb him the shelf was never dusted. He lived on the moths and flies that the lamplight attracted, but where he got his fluid from we did not know. I suppose he took a little stroll each night when the family was asleep. But for all the years as children when we visited Grandma, the tucktoo would make his nightly call. We never wanted to go to bed till he had tucktooed first. It was our bedtime call. Grandma used to say that the number of times he tucktooed was the number of years he had lived. To us he was ageless.

Mealtimes. These were always an occasion. Especially in Insein at Grandma's. Food was God's gift to us and meals as such were not to be taken lightly. They were to be set aside and savoured and given thanks for, she maintained. And so it was. Of course this was only during the holidays. When it was school time breakfast wasn't deemed an occasion. *Chota* it was called, and we had the midday meal at school. But evening dinner was a time when the family sat down together. We always started with soup, then a side dish which consisted of meat and vegetables, then a dessert. Lunch was a bigger meal in the holidays with a dish of curry and rice thrown in. But dinner was the formal time, when we had to be scrubbed and clean and on our best behaviour. This was between 7 p.m. and 8 p.m. Until we learned better, we used to leave the juiciest bit for the last mouthful only to be told we must leave it as it was bad manners not to leave a morsel on the plate. My Aunt was a stickler for this and she watched us with an eagle eye. It was not polite to clear the plate and give the impression that we hadn't had enough. We were very careful after that.

As for Grandma, Granny and Mr Walker? They were the despair of our poor *Ayah*/cook. Their false teeth fitted none too well, so before meals they removed them. Not when we had company though! And when they complained that the meat was too tough, our *Ayah* would throw up her hands in despair and say, 'You take your teeth out, so what do you expect! Go put them in again.' It amused us greatly because we thought Grandma's gums were a great deal tougher than her teeth. And it said much for the relationship we had with our *Ayah* who could speak her mind when she was in the right and no one would say a word. There was a very special feeling to those evenings, formal though they would seem to many today: the table laid in a gracious manner, with the pure white tablecloth beautifully laundered: the cutlery shining, and candles lit, the bone china plates and dishes and each course served in its turn.

The smell of the food, the gentle munching of the adults as they battled without their teeth, and we kids 'savouring' each mouthful. Those were wondrous days, and a time we thought would never end. The house would stand for ever, Grandma could never die, life would always go on with us kids dreaming and the dreams coming true. That life never stands still and that the future was not in our hands was not something my brothers and I were concerned with then. We just loved the life we had the love we were shown and the warm feeling of security we had with our Grandma.

Then there was bathtime. In our own home we had a bathroom with what we called an 'English bath'. Porcelain, large – very large – and we would fill it to the brim and dive in at the end. We also had a shower. But that was in one of the houses we lived in. Not so at Grandma's house. We didn't have electricity and we didn't having running water. But we had a well: deep, clear water which was fed from a spring and never dried up.

In Burma and later in India when we went to boarding school bathtime took place each day from 4 p. m. Each and every day we bathed. It was a ritual and we changed into fresh clothes for the evening. No one would dream of wearing the same clothes that they had worn during the day.

But of course, living in a hot country made having a bath each day common sense. Though in Grandma's house, even bathtime was not the same as elsewhere. Firstly our *mali* (the gardener) had to draw the water from the well and heat it. This he did over an open wood fire using the large tin containers the kerosene oil came in for the lamps and stoves etc. They were about two foot square (I think!) and made excellent water carriers. In the bathrooms were huge *chatties* – earthenware pots – which held cold water. These *chatties* came in all shapes and sizes and kept water cool even on the hottest day. The bathrooms were on a slightly lower level than the rest of the house

– five steps down! – and the floorboards had an even bigger gap than those of the rest of the house. Underneath the house there was a concreted area onto which the water would fall and a drain from there led into the surrounding forest. Actually I remember a huge clump of bamboo trees standing there. So all we had to do was stand on a little platform and pour the water over ourselves. Very efficient, and that was that. Bath times were very riotous and we could splash as much as we liked – no mopping up was needed. No cleaning of bath tubs no fuss. Great!

Then we dressed. White socks, freshly whitened shoes – does anyone remember Blanco? – a clean dress for me and for my brothers short trousers and shirt, and very inhibiting to us kids all this was. Then it was time for the evening walk, the grown-ups leading. Grandmas smelling of 4711 eau-de-Cologne, the rest of us smelling of baby powder. We would walk down the sea-sand road and towards the main roads in Insein itself and civilization: in other words, all the people who lived in the other houses in the area. We would meet the other kids who were also spruced up and it was a sore trial to them also, and while the grown-ups met and gossiped we children would kick up the dust with our shoes and be bored to death. We all longed to have a rough and tumble, but after bath time it was time to behave like little ladies and gentlemen and we didn't dare do otherwise. Yet looking back it was good discipline for my brothers and me, and we can thank our parents and Grandma for that. It was a habit we kept up and even now, bathtime and then eating family dinner together still prevails within the family. I call it a habit, but it is something that brings a sense of order to the day. It is like dividing the working day and the coming home and the end of the day as separate and cherished times.

But I must leave Grandma's house for now. As it figures all through my childhood in Burma you will hear more of it. What I want to tell you about now is 'my own self's house.' If I loved Grandma's house, this house was like my green hill and very special to me.

CHAPTER TWO

My Own Self's House

IN THE PREVIOUS CHAPTER I told you that when I was born, the doctor took one look at my scowling face and said to my Mother, 'You're going to have trouble with this one.' And I suppose that must have been the case for I never seemed to do anything right. Mother says I was contrary. She would say do this, and I would do that. I must have been a very trying child. But I couldn't always understand why I was being asked to do certain things which seemed unreasonable and made no sense! For instance: wool next to my skin would make me itch, and it still does so today, so I never use wool if I can help it. But as a child on one occasion, the grown-ups were feeling cold while we were seated outside at a friend's house, and they decided I too was feeling cold. I wasn't, but my Aunt insisted I put on a cardigan. Wool! I protested! But I was held down and the cardigan pulled on. Grandma was absent on this occasion or this would not have happened. My rebellion was reported back to Mother and of course it was my contrariness that was blamed. But life had many compensations. There were my brothers, and there was Grandma, and there was Father. Dear lovely Father who used to put me on his lap when things had been particularly bad and make me feel wanted and loved again. Mother says that I was a problem from the day I could walk and talk and think for myself.

At least for the first year of my life I was no problem. According to my sisters I gave them a great deal of pleasure. They were at the mothering stage and I was very ready to be mothered. Photographs show that I was a beautiful baby, so what happened later I have no idea because as I mentioned before I was considered 'plain'. Mother had been very ill after I was born so my *Ayah* looked after me. Oh, how I loved my *Ayah*! She was plump and sweet and was always there for me. Her hair was parted in the middle and pulled back tight into a bun, and she always smelled sweet and newly washed. I remember her back sometimes hurt and she would get me to walk up and down her back. A form of massage really and I wasn't very heavy or big and it helped her. She was very long-suffering and so good-natured. To lose her would have been unbearable, and I think this is true of most children who have 'nannyies' or *Ayah*s.

There was a deep attachment to my *Ayah*, and I think if parents who hand their children over to the care of these dedicated women realized to what extent a child gives of their love to these people, they would not be too sure of their hold on them in the love stakes. I loved my parents, but it was my *Ayah* I always turned to as a child when I was hurt or afraid.

In 1931 when I was just over a year old, we moved to a place called Malagong. If Insein had a special place in all our hearts, the house in Malagong had a very special place in mine. I called it 'My Own Self's House'. Even today I dream of it, and I am always searching for it in those dreams and I never find it! I always wake up infinitely sad. It wasn't as though there was anything extraordinary about it. It was a square wooden structure with a large sitting room with tiled floors and an archway leading into an equally large dining room. Stairs led up from the sitting room to a landing, then continued up into a large central room with large bedrooms on either side. The bathrooms lay off the bedrooms at the back of the house and these led onto a veranda. The wall in the front of the house upstairs was constructed of venetian shutters from top to bottom. We had a big window but even that had venetian shutters. As children we could sit on the floor, open the shutters and have a full view

Author with Ayah.

A Burmese cargo boat.

of the tennis court which lay outside and also watch the thunder and lightning and rain during the monsoon season.

It was in this house that I took my first steps, spoke my first words. My first remembrance of life, so it was natural the house in Malagong should be the most familiar and loving of all the houses we have lived in. The house was part of an estate called Minus's Estate or Coffee Grove. It lay on the banks of the Rangoon Creek which led into the Rangoon River. It was a factory estate and huge *godowns* (large corrugated iron sheds) stored sacks of paddy. These bags were brought into the estate by train, and stored till they were taken down the river by barge.

There were also open-sided *godowns*, where Burmese women worked. I am not sure what exactly they did, but it was something to do with sorting soya beans. I do not remember them being there all the time, so the work must have been seasonal.

But I do remember their chatter and laughter. They would have their children with them, and their babies. These slept in hammocks made from their mothers' *lunghis* (tubular ankle-length shifts that the Burmese women wear like skirts) slung between the posts of the shed. There they would lie happily gurgling. When they were hungry, they would be placed at the mother's breast and she would go on working. No fuss. No bother. The first rule of nature: when hungry – eat! I never heard howling squabbling children. The mothers in Burma, India and elsewhere in the East always kept their little ones by their sides – at least they did then – and family life was important. The elderly were respected and revered and taken care of, no old people's homes and children felt secure. That was then, but human greed and hate has changed all that; but that is not part of this story.

As for us? We were now a gang! Two other boys on the estate had joined us three. Victor and Freddie. Freddie was Tucker's age, and every bit as tough and untidy as he was. Neither of them ever looked anything but grubby, even in their Sunday best they somehow managed to transform themselves into a scruffy pair. Tucker today is very well groomed! Their knees were perpetually covered in scars, and they were always joking and getting into endless trouble. I have to admit being placed in the same category. I had straight golden hair and so had Tucker. Both of us had fringes, and as Mother always kept my hair cropped, and in the holidays and weekends I wore shorts, from a distance no one could tell who was who. Which didn't always work to my advantage – as I said before, my beloved brother could talk himself out of anything, and I couldn't. But all five of us were about the same height, very tough, thin and wiry and danger was not a word that came into our minds. Concern for life and limb didn't deter us from doing some of the things we did, and our respective parents would have spent a lot of the time on their knees had they seen some of the things we got up to.

But Alan and Victor! These two were the sane gentlemen of the group. Vic was my age, Alan was the oldest of us all. Where we were reckless, they were cautious. Where we were scruffy, they always managed to remain clean. While we got spanked they didn't. They were the restraining influence – at least they tried to be. No cut knees, no black eyes. Though Victor did land on his head once when we were playing leapfrog and as I went over him his knees gave way. He recovered but somehow I got told off by his sisters who mothered him and sometimes smothered him. But our Vic was a lot tougher than they realized.

We remained a gang for many years, only parting when we were sent off to boarding school. But while we were at Malagong, we were the only young children on the estate and felt

The gang. Left to right: Tucker, Victor, Freddie and Alan.
Grace at front with Gemmy.

a certain proprietary claim to it. Any visiting children came as 'guests'. They played by our right. We even felt rather proud, for the estate was guarded. Huge double gates led into it, and barbed wire surrounded it. Gurkhas guarded these gates and patrolled the grounds at night. This made us feel important, though as a gang, we never bullied or fought with others. Life was too good, and we were very good-natured and felt truly loved and cherished, so we extended the same courtesy to others.

We had the run of the place, and a massive run it was too. Apart from these huge *godowns* and open sheds there was one place which was a ruin. It had been a machine shop of some kind in the past, but was not in use any more. The roof had caved in, and the floors had gaping holes in them. The machinery was rusty and chunks of metal and iron girders lay around. We treated this spot with respect for we felt that if we accidentally touched one of the buttons everything would start working. Sheer imagination, but it was enough to keep us away from the place. I remember how it affected us when for the first and only time we went through it. We were very careful and silent, the vast machinery it seemed, watching us. None of us went though the place again.

Sometimes, loose paddy husks lay in vast piles beside other well-stocked bags of rice. When this happened we used to climb to the tops of the bags and leap into the pile of husks. It was tremendous fun even though we would come out scratching and itching like mad. We would spend the day rollicking in this fashion. I realize now the risk we were taking, for we might easily have suffocated in a pile too deep for us. If children ever needed guardian angels we five did. As I believe in them, I believe we did have them on duty there.

On the days when the paddy was to be taken down the river we would be up bright and early. It was the only time our respective parents knew for a certainty that we would not be getting into trouble. For we would spend the whole day sitting on the bank watching the coolies at work. Two narrow planks would be stretched from the barge to the bank of the creek, and the coolies would walk up and down, up and down, all day, never breaking their rhythm carrying the heavy sacks on their backs. Up they would go, dump them in the hold where other men stacked them, and then down on the second plank, to start again. In a constant stream like mechanical toys. The sweat would be running down their backs and faces. All they wore were loincloths, and some of them looked so thin we thought they would surely drop their loads. But they never did, and their spindly legs had more strength in them then ours ever would.

We would watch them all day, and all day the planks would be bouncing up and down in perfect time with the men's feet. The planks and the feet knew exactly when to meet each other and it fascinated us. We wondered what would happen if the rhythm was broken, or if the plank would do a double bounce at the wrong time. But it never happened. These men were so sure-footed and they never looked down. We kids asked if we could have a go once but the plank didn't respond to us and we ended up on our bottoms, legs on either side of the plank, and edging our way back to the bank. Our respect for those coolies doubled.

There was only one real danger in Malagong, and that was snakes. Cobras mainly. We would never venture out at night without a torch or lantern, and we never put our shoes on without giving them a shake first. This was second nature to us and we did not worry in the least. We had been taught to be careful and what to do in an emergency if we were bitten. Our Indian *mali* had his own cure, and he had been bitten three times. Apart from using herbs, he used to run and run and run. To a western doctor this would be the last thing one should do, but our *mali* survived. 'Keep the blood going round and round missy baba,' he would say, 'and then all the poison comes out in the sweat.' He had a point. But when a nest of cobras lived on our doorstep Father had to take drastic steps to get rid of them.

In one corner of our garden stood a banyan tree. This is a tree with a peculiar characteristic. Its roots spread themselves all over the ground, over and under and in great knotted gnarled lengths. It is a notorious habitat of snakes. So when we killed three cobras in quick succession father decided that the banyan tree needed investigation. And he was proved right. The tree had to come down, and they are very large so it was quite an undertaking. It was a dreadful shock for all – for there among the roots was a colony of cobras, hatched and unhatched. There must have been hundreds. Mother was horrified. We were used to snakes but had never seen such a thing before. What was the right method of killing them? They had to be killed immediately for now they had been disturbed they were beginning to stir and there was no way we could have killed them with sticks alone. So buckets and buckets of boiling water was poured into the nest. I know it seems harsh, but it was better than pouring petrol onto them and setting fire to the whole nest. Water and fire! Both can save and kill, and even today I hate killing in any form, animals and all life forms. But anyone who has ever seen death by snake bite knows that killing these snakes was a must. Apart from us kids, there were all the children in the *godown*s and the snakes would have headed for the sacks of beans and what would have happened doesn't bear thinking of. But even that was not the end. For the parent cobras were still at large, and father and a couple of Gurkhas sat up that night and waited for them. They were killed with *dundoos*. These are heavy sticks. We didn't kill snakes for pleasure or because they were dangerous, for usually they would slither away when humans were around. But this nest was literally on the doorstep.

I make Malagong sound a highly dangerous place. It wasn't. It was lovely, and we were free and happy. I had a cot in my parents' room. It was very large and the sides came down, so that as I grew it was no longer a cot but a bed. It was tucked into an alcove and as the room was very big I had my own little corner. And of course I had a mosquito net, as we all did. So it was very cosy, especially when the rain came down. A bit like Grandma's house then! Over the head of my bed I had a picture I loved, and it lived for me. It was of a little girl and boy picking flowers at the edge of a cliff. Behind them stood a huge angel with his arms stretched out. I knew then that they wouldn't fall – he wouldn't let them. That picture came alive for me every time I looked at it, which was every night. No picture has ever remained static for me, but I don't suppose it does for most people. I can visualize the next frame, and in my picture I could see the two small children moving very close to the edge and the angel ready to hold them if one of them slipped. I knew then with great certainty that I too had an angel. And if I wanted to go to the bathroom at night, I always said, 'I'm coming out now' just in case I stood on his feet. Fanciful? Maybe. But very real to me.

Even at this early age I kept my private dreams, my private 'knowledge' to myself. I did not know the Bible then as I know it now or that angels were real created beings, and figured greatly in Bible history. I had only my childish logic and intuition to lead me. Though I did know the story of Jesus and his birth affected me. Christmas and Easter were blessed times for us children.

At Easter, a large group from the church with the Pastor leading us would go, before the dawn, to the Kokine Lakes. We had a huge cross with us. And we would all stand silently as the sun rose over the water and the sky would be a riot of different colours. Then we would all sing the favourite hymn, 'Low in the grave He lay, Jesus my Saviour', and then leading into the wonderful chorus,

> Up from the grave He arose
> With a mighty chorus for His foes
> He arose the victor from the dark domain
> And He lives forever with His saints to reign
> He arose! He arose! Halleujah! Christ arose.

My father used to carry me. Early memories were vague apart from the rising sun, but later as I grew older, I too knew the words of the hymn, and as we sang, it seemed to me that all the angels joined in and the empty cross we carried said it all. The rising sun spoke of His majesty and touched the cross with red. My heart would beat faster and I knew – I just knew that Jesus was indeed alive. I thank God for a family who told me and taught me from such an early age, about Jesus. Even today, I find the Bible the most exciting, adventurous, compelling and challenging book I have read. And I have read hundreds of books. To me it contains every aspect of human frailty and strength, of deep abiding love, of warning too, and of righteous judgment. And of an enemy who seeks to destroy all that is good and honest. But Jesus! Ah! He could do anything.

Our church in Rangoon was a Methodist church but always had American Pastors. My Great-Grandmother had turned the first soil in the service of consecration before building started. The church was in the shape of a cross, with beautiful wooden pews. Not the kind that cut the thighs off halfway, but nice deep seats. When I was about six years old, a visiting evangelist called Mr Gaddis came to the church. I have no hesitation mentioning his name for he has long gone to be with his Lord and he was a man of true faith. This was a healing service also. I was placed in the right hand arm of the church and told, 'Now Gracie, don't move from this place'. I don't remember Alan and Tucker being with me. So there I sat as the church filled. My parents were helping seat everyone. What a service! A lot of it is very vague naturally, but some things are printed on my mind. Firstly there was the singing. I learnt four songs that day which I have never forgotten. But it was what happened at the end that even today lives on in my mind clearly. I suppose others were prayed for, but I only remember this one man. He was carried in on a stretcher and placed in the front. He couldn't walk and was paralysed from the waist down. Mr Gaddis just took his hands and said, 'In the name of Jesus, stand and walk'. And the man did just that. There was quite a stir in the church, and many didn't believe and said it was a put-up job and the man really could walk etc. This I learnt many years later. Miracles don't happen, people say. To my six-year-old mind this was normal for I already knew in my mind that Jesus could do anything. I just sat there happy and contented. Mother told me years later that the man was Burmese and had never walked. He was twenty-seven years old at the time. Many tried to prove it was a hoax, but his family and friends knew better. I can still see that man's face – he had come from death into life. Children do see things clearly, and as Jesus said, 'Unless you come as little children ...' I believed, I still do and that is that.

There was one very horrifying thing that happened in Malagong that no one on the estate ever forgot. My brothers and I certainly never did. In the East one has to be very careful. We are brought up never to touch other people's animals or animals one doesn't know, because of a disease called hydrophobia, or rabies as it is known worldwide. The fear of rabies is great and feared. If a friend's dog gets affected, everyone is told who may have had contact and appropriate action taken. With an unknown animal one never knows, so the command is, 'don't touch', for the germ can enter through even a small cut. If one is bitten, they must have the injections at once. These are given into the stomach, twenty-eight injections, one each day. Very painful and not a day must be missed. It is probably different today. But the injections are better than the disease. For it is a slow death, agonizing and ending in madness. A human being turns into a wild animal. All children no matter how small are aware of this, and the quarantine system in England has kept this country clear, and we should be grateful for it. But a lady on the estate had a dog which contracted rabies and bit her. She was a Christian Scientist or maybe a Jehovah's Witness – one or the other anyway – and refused to have the injections. Her husband ran the estate and they were a lovely couple. When her dog went mad, we kids were kept indoors till it was caught and shot. Without the injections and within the week this lady was rabid herself. My Mother stayed there to help, and we were so scared because we thought what would happen if she bit

Mother? On the night before she died her screams could be heard round the estate and we buried our heads in our pillows. The three of us huddled together and prayed for it to stop and please God look after our Mother. Then it stopped and Mother and Father returned home tight-lipped and white-faced. We never would forget that night. The cure was there but her religion forbade her to have the injections. God gave man the knowledge to fight these diseases and it is stupid of us to spurn the help it offers.

My second eldest sister had a cat called Jemmy. She was forever in the family way. One set of kittens she had were memorable. There were only two. One we called Twisty because he was deformed. He had a crooked neck, a crooked foot and a crooked tail, but he didn't seem to mind. But Tucker put some custard on the floor for the two kittens and then slipped on it. Unfortunately he landed on Twisty. We howled far into the night for that little kitten and the next day gave him a funeral fit for a king. The other kitten was given to my eldest sister who called him Puck. He grew into a beautiful cat who didn't know any better. He waged war on another tom-cat who ruled the district and was a terror. Puck took up the fight on behalf of all the other cats. I rather suspect they had the same father, but they were not to know that and were sworn enemies. Night after night Father went out with a bucket of cold water, threw it over the two warriors and then brought Puck home in the bucket. One night Father wasn't home and Puck did not return. So we went looking for him. My sister broke her heart for the cats had fought to the death. The other cat was dead, and Puck horribly mauled about. She nursed him and wept over him, but it was no use. Brave Puck died and the family went into mourning. I had always been the chief mourner and undertaker (don't ask me why) but I didn't want to bury Puck. But we eventually did, alongside little Twisty. And placed a slab of stone over the grave with their names written on it. We never kept any more of Jemmy's kittens after that. It was too painful.

It was there in my own self's house that I first walked. And it was there that I first went down the stairs by myself. I remember it well. When I told mother I remembered it well she said that I could not possibly have done so for I was barely eighteen months old, but I related the conversation she had with *Ayah* when they found me at the bottom and she admitted that that was indeed what they had said and she had never ever told anyone for one doesn't repeat all the conversations one has each day. It happened like this. I had been left upstairs, quite safely as a rule, but someone had forgotten to close the gate at the top of the stairs – the gateway to adventure – and I crawled to the open gate. It seemed an awful way down to the first landing, but I decided to have a go. I was in a nappy and a vest – barefoot. I turned round to go down backwards, but as I couldn't see where I was going decided that was a bad idea. So I turned round and holding onto the banisters with my left hand I proceeded to go down on my bottom, one step at a time. I was very careful, each move carefully thought out. Two feet on the step, bottom following till I reached the landing which was rather large. Then there were a further five steps to the sitting room. I had got this far, so I crawled to the top of those stairs and bumped my way down. Alas, the tiles were cold and all the shutters were closed, so it was dark. This I did not like and started to bawl. My cries brought Mother and *Ayah* running, Mother picking me up saying, 'Oh my baby, she's fallen down the stairs', and *Ayah* replying, 'No Mem-sahib, she won't have got round the landing if she had'. And of course I wasn't hurt – just scared. Lesson learnt? No way! Once I had got over the initial shock, I was raring to go again. But the gate was locked, and it was only when I could stand and undo the bolt myself that I was again able to take a trip downstairs by myself.

It was also at Malagong that Tucker nearly had his head split wide open with dreadful consequences. We were digging for worms. At least, Alan was. He was using a *mumpti*, which is a sort of spade with the spade part going at right angles to the handle instead of straight. One used it with a swinging motion overhead. Tucker spotted a worm and dived for it the same moment Alan was bringing the *mumpti* down. He had the presence of mind to turn it so that the head and not the blade hit Tucker's head. Bad enough! Blood everywhere. I didn't know anyone could have so much blood in them. Mother stopped the bleeding eventually. I suppose he had to have stitches but I don't remember that bit, all I remembered was wondering how were they going to put all that blood back into him? Surely he couldn't live with half a supply. Where would it come from? It really bothered me, and was yet another lesson I learned. Don't leave children wondering and worrying about things. Tell them!

Next to the house was a tennis court separated from the house by a huge trellis fence. I don't know that it was ever used except by us kids to play around in, for tufts of grass grew through the concrete cracks. There was a large tree which grew at the side of it and like the corrunder bush at Grandma's, I have never seen the like of it again. At certain times of the year it would have huge yellow puffballs on it. They would eventually fall off and we'd play with them. Hard on the inside, they were covered with this yellow soft stuff. Very strange and beautiful. I would hold them and wish to keep them forever – but of course they withered eventually. It's like beauty one sees everywhere. Clouds, a sunset, a rainbow, a beautiful flower or a moment of happiness one wants to hold onto for ever. I wanted to hold onto beauty like that, and as a child I had a deep ache inside when it passed and was gone. How can one capture a colour or a perfume or keep a beautiful moment forever? As I grew older and even today I can recall those treasured memories and realize that I hadn't ever lost them. They would remain with me always.

Another family on the estate were wonderful. It was John from their family who used to carry me on his shoulders when on holiday (that I will relate later on in the story.) His sister was married and had a little baby girl. I used to go and play with her until I was banned from going near her over an incident which was not my fault. No one believed me of course. It happened like this. She had a small tambourine which she loved playing with – it had bells all the way round the rim which made a lovely sound. On this awful occasion she decided to put it on her head and pull it down. The *Ayah*'s back was turned, so she didn't see what had happened. Of course the thing was round her neck and no one could get it off. It is such an easy thing to do, and we have all experienced the same thing. Put your hand in a bottle then try getting it out! But I got the blame. I was in dreadful trouble – real trouble. They said the child couldn't have done it. But I knew she had. She simply put the thing on top of her head and pulled down, I can still see it happening. My father and brothers believed me, but no one else did. I was called a naughty mischievous child (not by nice John though) and banned from going near her again. I loved that little child and missed her greatly. If only she could have spoken I think she would have stood up for me. But by the time the grown-ups had finished she was bawling her head off. Ah well!

The time at Malagong was a blissful time for the gang. We were too young to understand the problems my parents had, but we did have to leave 'my house' from mid-1934 until 1935, a year I will tell you about later. For Father had a very hard time. He was Motor Transport Officer for the Rangoon Corporation when we returned in 1935 and to go to his office was always a thrill. His Burmese drivers loved him and he did something for them which put his life at risk, something they never forgot. It isn't necessary to go into detail here and I certainly understood nothing then. But there were those who would have him dead, and a trap was set. He was ambushed and attacked violently and left for dead. The bone above his left forehead had been crushed with an axe, and when Father was found and rushed to hospital, they gave him no chance at all. But the surgeon operated and removed the splintered bones, and found none had penetrated the brain. Truly a miracle! Father always wore a soft hat after that, for though no one would have guessed he had an injury, he was conscious of his 'soft spot' and the need to protect it. After this attack others were attempted but his drivers would never let him go to any lonely spot on his own. And from then on Father always carried his revolver. Licensed of course. It was this revolver that was to save his life.

Riots between the Burmese and Indians flared up occasionally. Also between the Hindus and Muslims. Being in the middle of riots is not a pleasant thing. On one occasion, Father's drivers came in and said riots had started on the outskirts of Rangoon, which meant they would soon be in the city itself. Father came to the school and the headmistress sent the children home.

Those close to the school walked, but those further away had to be taken by car. But it had to be done fast. And sometimes some of the children just had to stay in the school till it was over. Father drove us. Malagong was also just on the outskirts of Rangoon and halfway home we remembered Beverly who came to school with us each day in my Uncle's car. We had left her behind. So Father dropped us off and headed back. We waited at home, all the doors locked and barred and the Gurkhas fully armed. We just prayed, and later we realized just how much those prayers were needed. For by now, the riots were in full flood. On his way back with Beverly six Burmese stopped the car. Dad told Beverly to lie on the floor in the back and he locked all the doors. These six men carried *dahs* – these are long wicked-looking knives or swords – and told father to get out of the car. He knew that both their lives would be worthless so he did the only thing possible. He leaned out of the window, and still keeping the engine running, told them that if they wanted him to get out they would have to take him out but he had a bullet for each of them. And if he was to go on the everlasting journey he would make sure they went with him. It was no idle threat, for my father was a crack shot and could hit centre from the hip. These six men believed him and gave way. Father put his foot down and broke all records getting home. He was shaking when he arrived. It was Beverly who told us most of it and she thought him marvellous. So did we!

During the riots the guards to the estate were doubled, for much looting went on. The Gurkhas carried their kukris with them. In the hands of a Gurkha they are more deadly than the Burmese *dah* for they are short and curved. With them around we felt a lot safer. As I mentioned earlier, the estate was surrounded by barbed wire. Outside our home and just outside the fence was a common path leading to the creek. On the same night that the six men held Father up, he stayed awake all night and kept watch. Rangoon was a dead and silent city and anyone venturing out would not stand a chance. But the rioting groups and small bands went around breaking into houses, well armed and ready for anything. Father knew only too well the methods they used and didn't want to be caught napping. My bed, being tucked into the corner of my parents' room, meant that as I drifted into sleep my last vision was of Father sitting at the window overlooking the path to the creek with his gun in his lap.

About three in the morning I awakened to soft voices and saw both Mother and Father peeping out of the window from behind the shutters. They were very still, and I sat up in bed and listened with them. Then I heard noises from outside and saw Mother put her hand to her mouth, and heard her whisper, 'What are we going to do Michael?' 'Only one thing to do,' he replied, crashing open the shutters, and in quick succession he fired his revolver into the night. Pandemonium! In a moment the whole estate was in an uproar, I had my pillow over my head and my brothers came and joined me in my cot. There were yells and running feet outside and Gurkha guards coming from all directions. What a night! The guards found a long plank resting against the fence, and some sacks which Father said they would have used to lay on the barbed wire. If Father had not kept watch those men would certainly have got over, and who knows what would have happened. For killing, looting and then burning was the usual practice of the rioters and if one sack in the *godowns* had had a match put to it, the whole estate would have been in trouble. Finally we settled into our beds again, except for Father. He quietly reloaded his revolver and sat down to keep watch again.

It was usually three or four days before it was considered safe to return to school. When one is little as we were, there was a sense of unreality about it. Nothing looked the same, felt the same or even smelt the same. As though the air we breathed had changed somehow. My own self's house was the only place in the whole world I thought where we could be safe. Even the night Father fired his gun into the air didn't make me afraid even though I put the pillow over my head. I still jump at the sound of a gun. Too young to realize the real danger we were in, my brothers and I were merely excited, even though we didn't dare go out, and for once my Mother knew where we were. I suppose it was the silence that affected us most. Everyone moved around quietly, everyone spoke in whispers – don't ask me why – and so we too went around like little mice. I can only describe it now as a 'fearful' silence!

There was another exciting occurrence for us, though not for the people concerned. It was the night the house next to Victor's caught fire. No one was in it at the time, but being all wood and in the dry season, it went up like a bush fire. Flames shot high into the air, and we all had to evacuate our homes in case the flying cinders set our homes alight also. The night was very warm and there was a breeze which did not help. Alan, Tucker and I had been bundled out of the house and into the car still in our pyjamas, and driven a safe distance away, while the fire brigade doused all the surrounding homes with water. The sight was terrifying and terrific! There was no hope for that house, and with no one being in the house the fire had taken hold before the smell of burning drifted through the windows of Victor's parents' home. Too late! We were beside ourselves with excitement. Middle of the night, fire engines all over the place. Not often one has a fire on one's doorstep, thank goodness. To us, another exciting happening, but not for the owners who came back to charred remains.

Yet another memorable time in Malagong was when the boys had new bicycles (not for me though!) It was a drastic decision for my parents to have made, and within two days my poor parents were sorry they had ever been invented. Being isolated in the estate, I suppose they thought the boys would learn to ride with no harm done. Firstly Tucker ran the *dhobi* over. If you think that impossible with a bike I assure that with my brother nothing was impossible. A *dhobi* is an Indian washer man. He would come each week, and he and Mother would sort the dirty clothes into bundles. Then he would fold each item and arrange them into a perfect square. This was placed into a sheet, and tied with a knot, and he would sling it on his back and off he would go. He would return a week later with everything beautifully laundered, still arranged in a perfect square. I don't think our underclothes and things like that were included. Just sheets and towels etc. Our poor *dhobi*, little did he know what was in store for him the day the boys had their bikes. He set off with his bundle of dirty clothes, not realizing that behind him came two little lads in the process of learning how to ride. And of course they were not looking where they were going. Alan, wobbling behind him, hit him square between his legs and the next minute he found himself in the air still clutching his bundle which probably helped him land unhurt. Barely had he hit the ground when Tucker ran right over him as he lay stunned and helpless in the road. Unfortunately it did not end there, for contrary to the laws of nature neither of my brothers had fallen off their bikes. Alan couldn't stop and ended up colliding with a gate, cutting one eyebrow so severely he had to have stitches. Tucker on the other hand rode his bike up a fallen lamp post – please believe me, he really did – doing irreparable damage to his bike, but not to himself. So what with an irate *dhobi*, a bloody Alan, and a 'I couldn't help it, it just happened' from Tucker, my parents were glad that both bikes were out of action. A sad day, which had started out so promising. No more bicycles – ever!

Malagong! Free and enchanted. At harmony with one another and never dull. School was to be tolerated, if only to humour the grown-ups. Tucker summed school up in a way only he could. His first day there made him very grumpy and he informed Mother he wasn't going any more. When asked why, he said, 'They don't know anything there, they're always asking me questions'. My brother Tucker! Our own world, of adventure, of secrets, and the future so far ahead that we had no wish to be grown up. Grown-ups were too complicated. Life seemed so simple really, so logical. All they had to do was enjoy life, as we did. But that's childhood, and all children should be allowed to have good memories. That we live in a world where so many do not have that is a terrible thing, and I thank God that before our world fell apart later, we did have this time. But changes come and my own self's house was to be no more. For first, Freddie's parents moved, then Victor's. And finally we did.

CHAPTER THREE

The Mota Sahib

WE SPENT ONE YEAR AWAY from Malagong. What happened to send us away I wasn't aware of at the time, but it was the year Father was between jobs. My two sisters had been sent to boarding school and the rest of us shared a house with some friends. Our quarters were rather cramped and at this time we didn't have a car of our own, the one and only time that we hadn't. But our Uncle Tom used to come and take us kids out to his home in Malagong, and the first thing we did was race back to my own self's house to see if anyone was living in it. And for that whole year, no one else did. And when things were sorted out we returned. Father was now Motor Transport Officer.

The owner had got the house ready for us. It smelled of new paint, and we now had electricity. It was wonderful to be back. I slept in my usual corner of the large room my parents had with my picture of the angel guarding the two children over my bed. I did not have that picture the year we were away. And Uncle Tom's car took us to school each day, for Father was not able to as yet. Uncle Tom's Burmese driver was very long-suffering with the three of us bouncing about behind him. We would urge him to go slowly to school, and overtake any car that was in front of us on the way home. My story overlaps in some ways with my first years in Malagong, and this second time there before we left for good. But this narrative would not be complete without our Uncle Tom.

Uncle Tom was the Foreman of the Burma Railways, and wealthy. He had married a widow with three children, but Aunt

Daisy was a third cousin or something so we were all related anyway. Both Uncle Tom and Aunt Daisy were large. Not fat, just very large. No floppiness about them at all. We three never saw them wobble as many fat people do. Uncle Tom weighed about eighteen stone, and all his men worshipped him and called him 'The Mota Sahib'. Big sahib! The word *mota* means fat, but that was not what they meant, because they thought his heart was as big as his body. So did we! We loved them both, for Aunt Daisy's heart was as large also. Through bad times they helped, and were always there for us. I remember how strong he was. He would hold out his arms, legs astride, and we three would hold onto his forearms and swing from them. We thought he was the strongest man in the world, and had he but known it, we would have taken on anyone on his behalf.

Another picture I have of him is sitting in the back of his car and filling the whole space. One of us would sit in the front, and the other two perched, one on each knee. No seat belts in those days.

On the occasions that I stayed there, I was allowed to roam at will. Their house was long with a portico running the length of it. At the back was a veranda leading off the upstairs bed-rooms. The back overlooked the maze of railway lines which was the terminus for all trains, especially goods trains, where the carriages and engines were maintained, and where goods were loaded and sent all over Burma. There was always much shunting around, with engines pulling and pushing, depositing carriages on one siding and then going to get other carriages. It was a constant source of delight to us and we would sit for hours watching the engines bustling around. We never tired of counting the length of the goods trains, and sometimes there was a derailment. Then Uncle Tom would take us to watch the huge crane as it lifted a carriage back onto the track. Great times!

This back veranda was a special refuge for me. When my Mother and I had an argument, which I always lost, I would say, 'I don't want to live in this house any longer'. Then no matter how I was dressed, be it in short pants and vest, I would pick up my potty, tuck it under one arm and march out of the house to go to Aunt Daisy. The Gurkha guards knew the scenario, so would make sure I crossed the main road out of the estate safely, and off I would go to Uncle Tom's house. It lay not too far over the main road, and when Aunt Daisy's servants saw me coming, they would go to her and say, 'Gracie baba has had a fight with her Mother again and is here with her potty under her arm'. 'Well you know what to do,' Aunt Daisy would say. The door would be open – we never closed our doors during the day in Burma – and I would march in, up the stairs and to one of the rooms upstairs at the back. There I would sit on the threshold and watch the trains. At lunchtime, the *chokra* (that is the boy who worked in the house) would put food near me, wordlessly, and I would eat it, then for the rest of the day just sit there in stony silence. Again at teatime. Then later in the day when Father returned from work, he would come and fetch me and with a 'humph', I would climb into the car, potty as well (I never did use it) and we would go home. No one said a word, including my brothers, and then I would go to bed, and wake up the next day as bright and sunny as always. What was going on in my head? And why did Mother have such a tussle with me? I do remember wanting to do things for myself and not being allowed to. 'You're too small,' was the usual response. Which was not logical to me at all, who wanted to try anyway. And also being told to do something which seemed silly. 'Go and sit down till dinner is ready.' Why? I wanted to know. My mind reacted to what seemed unreasonable, and with my own children and grandchildren today, I try to see things through their eyes and how I saw things as a child. Then things fall into place. It is easy to be wise after the fact, but if personal experience teaches us nothing, then we will go on making the same mistakes others have made before us.

Uncle Tom's and Aunt Daisy's house was a happy house. Large shadowy rooms in the front and bright rooms at the back. One room was rarely used. I suppose it was the drawing room for special occasions. I used to tiptoe in and sit in an angled sofa which was set against a wall. Venetian blinds were kept drawn and I would feel the silence in there, as though the rest of the house respected this room and who was I who dared to venture in? Yet I loved being in there. I have always loved silence. It is then when all is quiet that my thoughts drift into all kinds of wonderful worlds of my hopes and dreams.

Aunt Daisy had a pantry upstairs in which she kept bottles of sweets and Chinese fruits, and Burmese delicacies. After lunch she would ask the *chokra* to bring them, and we would have a choice. I've tasted those same things elsewhere but they never had the same taste somehow. We used to sit there with her, for she had a sitting room upstairs with large open windows overlooking the railway lines. I didn't know till later that she had a weak heart, which was why she spent so much time upstairs.

Dinner with them was a feast of lovely food. A long table laid beautifully in the downstairs dining room. Always on the table was a bowl of toothpicks (we used them to spear peas and corn with), and beside each plate was a finger bowl, and the water always had a nice smell – I know now it was rose water. At the end of the meal everyone would delicately dip their fingers in and the *chokra* would come around with a small hand towel and we would dry our hands. Very formal but we loved it! Even now my mouth waters at the thought of the food in Burma.

It was at their home that we had our smallpox vaccination. Mother says I was too young to remember for I was only two. But as I remembered my first venture down the stairs, I remember this too. And I remember it was painful. It was done in the closed section of their porch, on a bright sunny day. The doctor had all his gadgets on a table and a lot of people were milling around. I think everyone, including those who worked for my Uncle, were being done. I remember feeling very scared and awfully small and hanging onto my *Ayah* for dear life. My turn came. In those days it wasn't an injection. You either had three little scratches, done three times in a vertical row, or what we had that day. This was a circular gadget which the doctor put on your skin and then turned it. Then the anti virus or whatever was put on. And three times he put it on my skin, pressed and twisted, not something you forget. I yelled! I remember yelling! I was totally outraged at what was being done to me, and can you blame me? And I remember being ill afterwards, and being unable to lift my arm. If no one believes me – then feel free to visit and I will show you the scars! My only consolation was that everyone was done, but my arm was very tiny, and my skin very soft and everyone else was older. Aunt Daisy provided cool drinks and food, but the place smelt of medicine and no one was hungry.

Uncle Tom had a monkey called Jacko. Not a particularly pleasant monkey, but devoted to my Uncle. One day something frightened him badly and he bit the first thing to hand, and that was my Uncle's leg, through to the bone. Poor Uncle Tom! Poor Jacko! For the monkey was very sorry indeed. But he wasn't put down, but sent to the Rangoon Zoo where he spent the rest of his life happily with other monkeys, and Uncle Tom used to visit. But the bite caused pain for a long time.

Then one day Aunt Daisy's clothes caught fire. She had a small paraffin stove in her upstairs room and how it happened I do not know. She put the flames out herself, but both arms were burnt badly. Our family doctor who was Japanese wasn't on call, so another doctor came. But she screamed in pain and said she would wait for Doctor Suzuki. He was a wonder with burns and when her burns had healed there were no scars. He did the same for me later which I will tell you about – but not now. But our precious Aunt, with her weak heart and I think she had dropsy, took ill and went into Dr Suzuki's private nursing home. I remember the day she died. It was Sunday, and we went after evening church. The year was 1937. Mother and Father went in, and came out looking very unhappy, and took us three in. Aunt Daisy looked so pale and ill, but her eyes lit up when she saw us. We kissed her and then left. Uncle Tom was there looking sad and lost. Mother stayed on, while Father drove us back to Malagong, and then went back to be with his brother. But Aunt Daisy died that night. So within a year we had lost three members of our family. My Aunt with the broken back, Granny and now Aunt Daisy.

Their house was never quite the same after that. When a well-loved figure who has brought so much peace and happiness into others' lives dies, they leave a space that cannot wholly be filled. Uncle Tom's eldest daughter looked after him then, but she was never so free with the sweets, and I think found us three a bit much, mainly because she didn't understand us in the same way her Mother did. Uncle Tom just buried himself in his work, but he was always kind and caring to us. That didn't change.

My memories of Uncle Tom and Aunt Daisy's house is still vivid today, and two songs which send my mind drifting back to that home is 'Danny Boy', and 'Oh for the Wings of a Dove'. Aunt Daisy had a gramophone, but this record was the only one I remember. Both songs were sung by a young boy with a beautiful voice. Clear and sweet. I wish I knew who that singer was. But oh the longing in my heart! To be able to sing like that – to be able to soar into the sky with the wings of a dove.

Heaven never felt nearer than those moments of listening to that lovely voice.

So that was the Mota Sahib. A man whose memory lives on for his love and kindness and generosity. My Uncle Tom!

CHAPTER FOUR

Lancaster Road

FOR ONE YEAR WE LIVED in Lancaster Road. It was the year between the first and second times in Malagong. We shared a house for this time, and as the school we attended was next door, we didn't have to get up so early. I was five going on six and school wasn't too much of a problem brain-wise, having two elder sisters and a passion for reading which I still have today. I learned to read at a very young age. I was no genius and would never claim to be as brilliant as my sisters who always shone in their studies, but words made sense to me. So being interested I learnt fast. Kindergarten was no challenge as a result. But I had a teacher, Miss Stacey, whom everyone loved. We had all been her pupils at the beginning of our school lives, and we would do anything for her. She believed in discipline, and she ruled us and taught us with firm but loving hands. Tucker was a rascal but in her hands he was putty. We owe a lot to her teaching and her kindness. She loved her job. She loved sharing knowledge with her children, and little as we were we sensed this in her and responded. We too wanted to hear and learn all we could. I did learn not to read just anything, but the things that would stimulate my mind, and make me inquisitive about the world and life in general. It was because of that very early guidance that I found world history and geography so exciting. And of course English literature. I shall always be grateful to her.

Another one of the kindergarten teachers was a lady called Miss Beal. She played the piano for us. I don't remember if she taught us anything else, but I was fascinated by the way she settled herself at the piano. She was a bit plump, and always seemed to wear shiny skirts, which were somewhat tight. We all used to watch as she pulled the piano stool out, sat on it and then got herself settled. This meant running her hands down the back of her bottom and down her thighs till her skirt was pulled smooth and down. Then she would wiggle herself into a comfortable position, take a deep breath and begin. What was so fascinating to us, was that there was never a crease in the bottom half – so to speak – of her skirt. It remained taut and tight and shiny, and she never moved at all. Once she was settled that was it. Remarkable the things one remembers! She did play the piano well though.

Our school was the Methodist Girls High School. And the church where my Great-grandmother turned over the first soil was part of the whole complex. Mostly day scholars, but there were some boarders too. It was called a girls' school, but up to a certain age boys attended also, so my brothers and I were not split up till later. My Great-Aunt Charlotte, whom I never knew, was one of the first headmistresses. But in the years we were there we had two in succession. The one I remember best was Miss Reid. A dear kindly soul and plump. It is quite possible at this stage that everyone looked plump to me, so it is more than probable they were not; in the same way that a child thinks their teachers are old when they are only in their twenties. Having said that, anyone who was sweet and kindly, I also deemed plump. Like my *Ayah*! No, I believe she really was well covered! From Miss Reid, I never got a spanking. But the next one who followed her was quite a one for spanking, alas! She used a cane, and it hurt. And for little reason we were sent to her. Teachers could only stand you in a corner and give you lines, but it was the head who did the caning! But we chosen few who made the trip to her study got used to the injustice of the whole thing and shrugged it off. We never told Mother though. It was possible that she would give us an added wallop, thinking we had deserved the caning in the first place.

The problem was very simple. We were English, truly English, and many of the pupils were Anglo-Indian or Anglo-Burmese.

Among true Burmese, Chinese or Indian children we had no problem, but for some reason the Anglo-Indians gave us a hard time. 'You're not really English,' they would say, 'you must have some Indian blood in you.' It mattered not to us, and we could never understand why it mattered to them. As a child it seemed so unfair that being English was such a drawback, even with one or two of the teachers. Hence canings we did not deserve. It would have been better to have been an Anglo-Indian, for being English was no help at all. Our friends didn't care of course, and I never saw a difference between anyone anyway. The Chinese were proud to be Chinese, the Burmese proud to be Burmese, and if you had a bit of all of them in you, I guess that was an added bonus. That's how I thought then and still do today.

The teaching was excellent, the teachers truly dedicated, and because discipline was adhered to, teachers had no problems as a rule. Disorder and answering back were things that we did not do. But children were greatly encouraged in the things they were good at. Also there was no streaming, which was a good thing. It was recognized that not all children were good in the same subjects. I was not brilliant at maths though I got by. So I sat near a girl who was and apart from tests or exams, she could help me if I got stuck and the teacher had others to attend to. But I was good at history and geography and biology so I could help others with those. No one was made to feel less bright than anyone else. Though some were! But even those were good with their hands, and in art. Also a child could start in one school and finish in the same, right up to the university entrance exams.

Unfortunately things changed for us as a family and then the war came. But at the end of the year before we went up to the next standard, we went up as a whole class, and all the teachers knew all the children. Nothing too traumatic as a result.

I was good at poetry – the speaking of it, which also entailed what I most yearned to do. Act! Each year we had poetry competitions between all the schools, and in three sections, juniors, intermediates and seniors. I was in the juniors of course.

This particular year – I was about eight years old – I had to recite, 'The King's Breakfast' by A. A. Milne. It starts, 'The King asked the Queen, and the Queen asked the Dairymaid, Could we have some butter for the royal slice of bread?' etc. But I very nearly didn't do it ... The night before, our *chokra* was about to serve dinner, and was bringing the soup to the table. It was boiling hot, and I ran full tilt into him and the boiling soup went over my right shoulder, across the back and a bit of my upper arm. I had third degree burns. The poor *chokra*, whose name was Pythulli, ran to my parents who were sitting on the balcony to tell them that Gracie Baba was burnt. Gracie meanwhile was standing under the shower and letting the cold water take some of the sting and pain away. I had not taken my dress off. There was not much to it anyway, just a cotton slip really, so when Mother found me, I was standing in the bath with the shower streaming down on me, and very much in shock. I was dried after a fashion, my dress cut off, and a soft quilt wrapped round me. I remember I did not cry, I just sat numb with pain and shock. Father rang our lovely Japanese doctor, and then I was carried to the car and taken to the same private hospital in which Aunt Daisy had died. He had treated her burns without leaving scars and he did the same for me. I remember the relief just from the pain receding. He was wonderful. But I had a poetry competition the next day. Mother had told the headmistress what had happened, and I knew that the juniors faced tough opposition, so I told Mother I was going to do it. I simply dug in my heels and that was that. I was taken back to see Doctor Suzuki the next day and he redressed the burn and said, 'You go and do it, Gracie'. So I did and, immodestly said, got full marks. But I think part of that was the fact that word had got around about the bad scalding, and I stood on the stage with cotton wool sticking out from my sleeve and neck. I was obviously heavily bandaged up, and at eight I was still a rather little skinny girl, who was pretty tough actually. Our gang at this particular time were all together again and as they never treated me as a girl anyway, I was as tough as the four boys, Alan, Tucker, Freddie and Victor. But I loved the attention I got from the family, especially my *Ayah,* and there was an added bonus! Every time I went to see Doctor Suzuki, he gave me a Cadbury's milk chocolate finger. He had a box full of them in a drawer which he kept for children. I have never seen them again done like this. Each chocolate finger was individually wrapped in silver paper, in different colours. I coveted the whole box, not for the eating of, but for the keeping of. The colours were so nice and shiny. Bless Dr Suzuki. I healed as Aunt Daisy had, smooth new skin with no discolouration at all.

There was a story book we had in our class, and one of the stories, with a picture as well, was about a man who had swallowed a seed, and a tree grew out of his head. I can still see that picture even today. Only a fairy tale, but at six my imagination took off. One day, I was eating a custard apple, and swallowed one of the seeds. I said quite happily to Mother who was in the bathroom, 'Mummy I've swallowed a seed'. And Mother without thinking said, 'Oh dear, have you?' And to me she sounded quite worried. Visions of this man with a tree growing out of his head floated through my mind, and I was sure that I too would have a tree growing out of my head. And a custard apple tree at that! It was weeks before I realized that it would not happen to me. Weeks of feeling the top of my head expecting any moment to feel a bump and waiting for the tree to start coming out. Sounds silly I know, but to a child these things can seem very real. Again I learnt something from this, and so I always explained even the most trivial things to my kids, so they wouldn't ever imagine the worst.

Granny died while we were at Lancaster Road. I remember that day so well, for my parents went off and left us in the care of our *Ayah.* In that 'between' year, she wouldn't leave us. So much a part of the family, she stuck with us through thick and thin.

Granny died that night at ninety-three years of age, and my parents didn't return till after the funeral two days later. There is a funny side to Granny's last illness. She contracted malignant malaria, and at that age didn't stand a chance. Granny was a teetotaller, and had signed a temperance pledge when she was sixteen years old. When the doctor prescribed brandy, Grandma was in a bit of a fix. 'she signed a pledge never to drink,' she told the doctor. But Mr Walker sensibly pointed out that as she had never tasted it, she would not know it was brandy. Give it to her and tell her it is medicine. So they did! And she loved it! My, how she loved it! But our Granny was no fool. She may not have tasted brandy, but she had certainly smelt it. And as taste and smell are connected, it wasn't long before Granny put two and two together. She demanded to know whether it was brandy. Grandma, expecting fireworks from her Mother, tried to hedge around it, but Granny said 'Tell me'. So Grandma admitted this was so as the doctor had said she had to be given it. To everyone's astonishment Granny calmly said, 'Just think what I have been missing all these years!' I think Granny died a happy and quite possibly slightly drunk old lady. Certainly she slipped away very peacefully.

The people whose home we shared for that year were old friends of my parents. The husband was a journalist and he used to do a cartoon strip each week in the *Rangoon Gazette* about a little girl called 'Merry Sunshine' and all her adventures. He used to sing the little ditty that went with it to me. It went like this:

> Good morning Merry Sunshine,
> Why do you wake so soon?
> You've scared away the little stars
> And you've driven away the moon.

Fortunately for me I did not know till I was very much an adult that Merry Sunshine's adventures were based on the things I got up to. Even to the fact that I would take off to my

Aunt's with my potty under my arm, when I had an argument with Mother. Apparently Merry Sunshine had quite a following. I'm glad I knew nothing about it.

This lovely man had two sons. One of them was a bit of a wimp, the other like the rest of us, but the former was always getting us into trouble. He was truly scared of just about everything. We called him a coward because we had to take the blame for so much he was guilty of. And his Mother always believed him. Poor lad! He would be shaking like a jelly at the thought of punishment, so often we would simply take the blame for him and put it behind us because in spite of it all he was quite likeable. Pathetic, but likeable! I wonder what happened to him.

I enjoyed school as a whole, but bullying was not tolerated in any shape or form. But the best thing about our school was the fact that the kids themselves would not accept bullying. The girls had a gang, and the boys had a gang, and we were rivals up to a point. But if any child was afraid of a another child then they had to face up to one or another of the gangs. We did not cause trouble or go looking for trouble, we were simply kids who got together to share and talk and have fun. But on one occasion there was a fight. The first and last we ever had between the gangs ... There had been a very bad storm and a massive tree had fallen in the school grounds. It was a wonderful object to play on. A huge trunk from which the branches spread out and made great jumping off places. Climb along the trunk and then swing to the ground from the branches. Great fun! But the boys decided to keep everyone else off the tree, and we girls really resented that. We too wanted to have fun on it! But they wouldn't let us. So it was decided that we would fight for the tree. They would choose a boy, and we would choose a girl, and the two would have a fight and who ever won, the tree would be theirs. They chose me, and a lad who I won't name here but whose name I remember very well. So the fight was arranged for after school on a special day. Talk about a boxing ring! Kids formed a huge circle, and there was this lad and myself in the middle. How old was I at that time? It was 1938 so I wasn't quite eight years old. My brothers had taught me to fight, and were on the sidelines to give me support – in a quiet way for they were part of the boys' gang and couldn't be seen to be on my side – and so the fight started. I was fast and strong, but we were well matched and wow! The noise, the yelling, the cheering – 'Come on Gracie' which my brothers couldn't refrain from yelling also – made it something no one could forget. Did I win? Apparently I did for the tree was ours. I had bruises all over, the other lad got a black eye, our clothes were in a mess – but oh, what a victory! And did we keep the tree to ourselves? No, we shared it with the boys. But we all learnt a lesson from that. It was better to share in the first place. No resentment either. We shook hands and that was that!

My brother Tucker had quite an experience too. There was a lad at school, another English boy, who had a beautiful set of front teeth. The two upper ones were rather protruding and large, but white and beautiful. My brother always used to run with his head down charging to wherever he was going, and on this occasion it was down one of the school's long corridors. This lad, Clive, happened to be in the way and Tucker went straight into him. Tucker's head collided with Clive's front teeth, and with a toss of his head Tucker broke free. Unfortunately the teeth came away also, imbedded in my brother's head. Clive stood there holding onto his mouth, blood all over, and Tucker stood there with Clive's two beautiful teeth in his head, and blood all over the place. It took a pair of pliers to get the teeth out of Tucker's head, and very nearly a court case for the loss of Clive's teeth. They were his second set. But it worked out well, for the replacement teeth did not protrude and Clive, who was quite good-looking apart from these two teeth, was greatly improved in appearance.

My two sisters were in the same school. Older than us, they were prefects, and highly thought of. Very clever, very good – I don't know that they ever got into trouble, not like us three. But they were our champions none the less. Every so often my eldest sister was sent for because of some misdemeanour on our part. But my sister knew us well. She knew that we never lied, and when in the wrong took our punishment. Often we were blamed unjustly, so when my sister was sent for she always heard both sides of the story and then would make her feelings known. Why the teachers ever sent for her I never knew for it was never to their advantage. But my sister was one of the best scholars that school ever produced, and she could be quite formidable too. We were very grateful for her. We missed them both when for the short time they went to boarding school, till our life in general was sorted out.

There are fond memories of this school, before I was sent off to boarding school. I never won many prizes for being a brilliant student, though I won the Scripture prize from the moment I could read. I had loved reading the Bible right from my earliest memories when I first heard the Bible stories from my parents. So I was always top of the class in that direction. Also for recitation. But the most promising pupil, the cleverest, the hardest worker, the best at maths etc, they never came my way. I passed all my exams when the time came, and I retain the knowledge I learnt at school. Later of course, history, geography and biology, as I said earlier, were the subjects I did well in. To be interested in something means one is willing to read about it.

There was one incident which was awful for me. I was only six at the time. Each class was to plant a tree for a reason that I do not remember to this day. But there was to be a big tree planting ceremony followed by everyone meeting in the school hall, with a child from each class saying a little poem. Another child was to do the poem from our class, and had learnt it. When the time came, this child didn't come to school that day. So the teacher said I had to do it, and I had one hour to learn it off by heart. She said I wasn't to go on stage with a piece of paper. I was not happy at all. I tried and tried to get it into my head in the very short time I had, and when the time came I was thrust on stage with all the others still protesting that really I didn't know it. My turn came, and halfway through I dried up, and my teacher didn't even try to prompt me. Kids in the front row started to laugh, and there was a very embarrassed silence. I got angry. I was there through no fault of my own, expected to learn a poem in a very short space of time, and now people were laughing. So I stamped my foot, and said in a very loud voice, 'Well if you can do better, come and do it!' And I marched off the stage. No one called me to task over that episode. When Mother heard what had happened she was furious with the teacher. I very nearly refused ever to do anything again, but later I was to do 'The King's Breakfast' for the school competition when I scalded my back. And that was to lead into my first ever professional job. I was asked to do it on 'Children's Hour' on Rangoon radio. 'Aunty Gwen' was the one who did Children's Hour, and had contact with the BBC and 'Uncle Mac' who ran things in London. We were able to get the BBC in Rangoon and vice versa. That was followed by a parody on 'The King's Breakfast' called 'Adolf's Butter'. I read that but have no recollection about what it was all about apart from the fact it was about a chap called Hitler.

Between all these comings and goings and happenings we moved back to Malagong, and then finally to Pagoda Road, from where eventually I would be sent to boarding school in a place called Maymyo. More of that later.

CHAPTER FIVE

Pagoda Road

W E MOVED FROM MY BELOVED HOUSE to Pagoda Road. Shoay Dagon Pagoda Road to be exact. The Shoay Dagon Pagoda lies at the end of the road, which is a straight road leading from the river. Trams run along it. The Pagoda itself towers above Rangoon. It is three hundred and seventy feet high and rests on a mound one hundred and seventy feet in

Shoay Dagon Pagoda seen from the Cantonment Gardens

height. The Pagoda is covered in gold leaf and it is a marvellous sight to behold when the sun hits it, especially in the evening. We lived not too far away and could always see the Pagoda.

Our house used to be an old Chinese hotel and was quite unique. We lived in the upstairs part, and an old (or maybe she wasn't so old) lady lived downstairs, which was divided in two flats. Freddie, one of our gang, and his parents lived in one of the downstairs flats. Victor's parents lived just across the road, so all three families ended up together again after leaving Malagong. Our part upstairs was huge. The house had a large portico over which was a balcony, equally large, where my parents would sit of an evening, and we kids would watch the stars at night and fireworks whenever there was a festival of some sort. More of that later. The house had two huge gates and a circular drive. We had a tamarind tree, a bale fruit tree and one other, the name of which escapes me at the moment, but I hope I remember it and tell you about it later.

Stairs led up through double doors downstairs and into a vast semi-circular room which had wide double windows all around it. The balcony led off this room. This semi-circular room was divided by two twin columns from a long corridor, off which led two extremely large bedrooms each with its own bathroom. One end of this corridor led past one bedroom and ended with huge double windows at the end and on one side. The other end opened into the dining room, again with huge windows. The walls and the windows were all made of shutters rather like at Malagong, so we were able to open everything up and let air circulate. Because the bedrooms were so large, both were divided up. Alan and Tucker had their own section, my sisters theirs, and I of course had my own corner in my parents' room. There was one very unusual feature which I have never seen in any house anywhere. In the two bedrooms, on the outside wall were shutters from the floor up and reaching to the window sills. These could be opened, and had vertical bars from top to bottom. I used to sit on the floor and look out into the next door house and garden. Very strange this was. Even stranger was the fact that next door was a dark strange

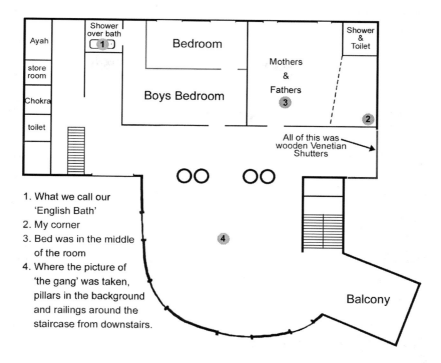

1. What we call our 'English Bath'
2. My corner
3. Bed was in the middle of the room
4. Where the picture of 'the gang' was taken, pillars in the background and railings around the staircase from downstairs.

house where the shutters were always locked. Our imaginations used to take off, especially so as the only movement that took place happened at night, and we never saw the people who lived there. It was the sort of place that we longed to investigate, but we felt sure we would never come out of again. Everything about the house we were in was unusual. The columns were like old Roman pillars, and though I call it a corridor it was just a wide open area which extended the length of the house. And from the dining room at the other end were large doors which led to the kitchen and *Ayah*'s and *chokra*'s bedrooms and the back stairs.

We now walked to school so we got home earlier than we had when we lived in Malagong and had the long drive home. I loved that walk each day. Turning right out of our drive, after about fifty yards there were crossroads. Turning left, and walking down that road – now what was its name? – I passed the GHS (Government High School) on the left and then right into Sula Pagoda Road. On the right was a beautiful white house with marble statues and a pool, which belonged to a very wealthy Chinese family. Hughie the son was at school with us, and a nice lad he was too. Then continuing down I passed first the church then turned into the school. Sometimes I went the other way, and past where we had lived for a year between the Malagong years. Sula Pagoda Road was a bit like Shoay Dagon Pagoda road, for it too ended with a pagoda. But Sula Pagoda was a third of the size, and the road went right round it. Trams and buses and cars, rickshaws and cycles were all fighting to get round it. A very busy street indeed, with the fire station, the cinema where I saw Shirley Temple in 'The Blue Bird' and the market which Mother used to take me to. Scot Market it was called. There was the Bonanza shop where the man always gave me a bar of Aero chocolate. I loved the holes in it, and would take ages over eating it. So many stalls crammed in – a bit like our closed markets here – but in many instances the shopkeepers would be sitting cross-legged on the same level as their goods. Especially the *dersies*. These are tailors. They would sit with all the material around them, and cut and sew on their machines and produce masterpieces! I could have stood and watched for hours. How I loved going to the market with Mother, it had a fascination for me I never lost. No market has ever had the same atmosphere for me. The men and women, Burmese and Indian, were always so kind and polite. They are courteous people, and I grew up, as my Father had, loving them. Burma is such a beautiful land, and I wish I could visit, but it is not the same today. There is so much strife and pain there now, which the people of that country don't deserve.

It was at a place called Rowe and Company that I bought my
teddy. Or rather it was bought for me. This was a huge store,
full of English goods and goodies. A great toy department which
I could only dream over, except this once. I saw him! My teddy!
Only about seven inches long. White, with a little squashed face,
and nice paws. His head could move round and so could his
arms and legs. How I wanted him! I felt he had been waiting
for me. But I didn't dare ask. Then for some reason, I have
never fully understood, Mother bought him for me. Perhaps she
saw the look on my face! I loved that little teddy and when
Burma fell to the Japanese Teddy never left my side. I hung
onto him, and where I went he went. He stayed with me over
forty five years. Then I let my husband take my treasured teddy
to sea with him. All was well, till he took Teddy out of his
briefcase and put him into his suitcase, and then on the way
back to his ship, he stopped to pick up some tickets and the
taxi driver took off with his luggage. This happened in Miami,
and I don't know where my Teddy is. Perhaps the taxi driver
let a child have him, or the worst I can imagine is that he was
just thrown away. My precious Teddy. My husband was not
able to pursue the matter, as the ship immediately sailed. Even
now I feel terrible when I think of that little bear. I understand
children crying over toys they love, and I could never call them
silly. For even now I miss my teddy. He had grown old with
the years, and I had to mend his paws, and I am sure he was
grateful. Also his head had to have a few stitches to keep it
firmly fixed to his shoulders, for the swivel mechanism had
failed. And his face looked more squashed too, but he was still
endearing. On one occasion on the ship, my husband gave him
a wash, and left him in a pail soaking, only to find the room
steward had pushed Teddy under the water. I think the poor
man thought that this particular officer was off his head for my
husband said, 'Don't do that, he'll drown'. How real can a teddy
get?

I also had a parasol. I still have it, and it is sixty-one years old. It still works too. It is a child's parasol made of flowered cotton. I lost my teddy, but I have the parasol. Though the love for my teddy was something special, in a way I care about this parasol too. When I first had it, I went into flights of fancy and imagined all sorts of things. I was a different person each time I opened it. Sometimes I was a little rich girl, at other times I had found it, or was given it, and each story had a different ending in which the parasol played a vital part. Not many things are left from my childhood in Burma. But the memories are there and they are treasured. As a child I kept so much locked away, so much that I found hard to share with anyone because I thought I would be laughed at. The feeling still exists all too often, but I find myself looking at kids and putting myself in their shoes, remembering what it was like for myself. Afraid of the blackness, feeling plain and skinny. Being accused of lying when I was telling the truth, taking the blame for others, being put down because I wasn't as clever as my sisters – but it was not their fault – and lying in bed tortured by the unknown at times, yet looking at my picture with the angel I would be at peace again. I was a happy child really. And always optimistic about things. I could always bounce back. Even though I considered myself unimportant and in a way lived in the shadow of my sisters, or so I thought at the time, I had the friendship and companionship of my brothers who I loved dearly and still do, even though Alan was lost to us a great many years later. It isn't often that such a bond exists between two brothers and a sister. My sisters were older than us, and when they were in their late teens, we hadn't yet entered ours and so in many ways there was no comparison between myself and them, but I was too young to understand things then. I only knew that I never got things right. Yet, I was still a happy child, which is the truth.

I mentioned earlier that we had what we called an English bath.

It was in this house. It was huge, and was free-standing. The floors of the bathrooms in this house were very smooth concrete with a drain hole. So any water spilt just ran away, rather like the shower cubicles we have today, only this applied to the whole bathroom floor. So the three of us used to fill the bath to overflowing – cold water of course in a hot country – and then used to dive in at one end and come up at the tap end. The bath took two lengths of me. Then having had a wonderful time there, we would soap the smooth floor and then skid about on it on our bottoms. The bathroom being large we could go from one end to the other, kick against one wall and go sliding backwards.

Zipping back and forth and colliding with each other and laughing our heads off. When Mother wasn't around we three would have a wonderful time. The bath had a shower over it – the same shower I stood under when I burnt myself – and this we would turn on full pelt. Water all over the place. Great!

We would eventually come out of the bathroom so clean – our faces would be shining, even though our eyes would be somewhat bloodshot with diving under the water. To this day I have never seen such a large bath tub.

With Victor and Freddie near us also, and being the gang again, holidays and weekends were a time of adventure. There were other kids around also, and we had a game called 'Kick-the-Can'. Very simple. Even our sisters and Victor's sisters would join in. There could be twenty or more of us. Invariably the game was at Victor's house for theirs was the largest garden. The game went like this. A tin can was placed in a circle, usually near a tree, and one person was 'it'. That person counted to ten, and all the others went and hid. The idea was that the 'it' person had to find us all, and call our names as he/she did so, and each time had to race back to the can and touch it before the person he had found, did ... Added to this, one person could save the lot merely by being the faster runner and getting to the can first, and kicking it. It didn't always work because it depended who could run faster, but if it did everyone was saved, and the poor person who was it, started again. Otherwise the first person caught had to take his or her place. As we played this at dusk, it was fun, but it was an unwritten law that no one would cheat by hiding too close to the can. It would not be fair on the person looking for us. A lot depended on the speed of each one.

And of course there was kite flying season. The kites we flew were made of strong tissue paper. They were flat and came in all sizes and colours. It is hard to explain how they were made. It's best to give a diagram, which I will do at the end of this chapter. All the kids had kites and many of them. And of course we all had rollers with handles onto which the string for the kite was. But we then had to make *munjar*. To do this we would get a bottle or a glass, put it in a cloth, and then pound it as fine as we could. This we would then mix with

Tucker, Gracie, Freddy, Alan & Victor on their favourite tree at 101 Pagoda Road, Rangoon, 1939.

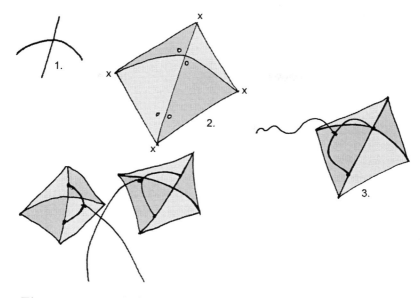

1. *Tissue paper with fine bamboo strips are used to form the cross.*

2. *The paper of the kite is then stretched around this frame and stitched along the edges, fastened at the points marked X. The kites are in different sizes and the colours vary. Striped squares, 4 oblong colours, a multitude of variety.*

3. *To fly them use ordinary machine thread, for the balance of the kite you make two tiny holes top and bottom you then take the thread though and form a centre point with the string or 'munjar' – you knot this at a point in the middle and hold it out until the kite balances horizontally. You will find the true balance by moving the point at which the main string joins the thread. Attach to the roller from which the action of the kite is controlled.*

cooked rice and paste. A very lethal mixture, which we would then coat the string with. We would put the string – and there was a lot of it for the kites flew high – strung out like a washing line, and then let the sun dry it out. The result:

razor-sharp string. There was a reason for all this. For there were competitions, to see who could cut the string of other kites, and send them flying away. When this happened there would be a shout of, 'Off he goes' and a horde of kids would chase the kite. Whoever caught the trailing string, claimed the kite. But it was a game of skill. Letting the kite go, crossing the other person's string, and then rolling in very fast, letting go and pulling in. The best won. Not all the string was made into *munjar*, because then kite flying would have been hard on kids who didn't know how, or were too young to make it. It was reserved for special times. But an 'Offego' as we called them had all the kids running in every direction, yelling.

Many a cut finger resulted from this, but it was a hazard all the kids accepted. The things we did!

It was in this house that we used to have a *Ponghi* – a Buddist monk – visit every so often. My father had saved his life (I have no idea what the circumstances were) and this *Ponghi* loved my Father. And we never knew when he would turn up. If Father wasn't home, he would just come in – we never locked the front door – and we would find him sitting on the sofa, cross-legged, with our dog Mary at his feet. He never spoke to us, only to Father. But our *Ayah* used to make him tea, which he loved and he would sit there and drink it quietly, and then as silently as he came, he left. It never worried us in the least, and we were never afraid of him. In his saffron robes and shaved head, we just accepted him as we accepted everything else in our childhood. It was all normal to us. I wonder what happened to him?

As a child I suffered from chronic bronchitis and I used to get very ill. On those occasions my temperature would rise and I would be coughing and wheezing and feeling very sorry for myself. Mother had something called Po-Ho oil (one can still buy it today) and this she would rub on my chest. I hated it, because it used to burn, and the smell would get up my nose and down my throat, which it was supposed to do – but I didn't like it and would pull the sheet up round my neck and feel more miserable than I already was. And it was bronchitis which kept me at home and from something I had loved for as long as I could remember ... Every Christmas our church would go out carol singing around Rangoon in an open lorry, and cars. A pedal organ was placed in the back and everyone carried lanterns. From place to place we would all go, and along the way there were stops at certain homes for refreshment. Then off we would all go again. A magical night, and usually quite a cold night too. It can be cold in December in Burma. From a tiny child I had been taken along and it was magical for my brothers and me. I was always wrapped up well in case I caught a chill. Then one year when I was about seven and a half I had a bout of bronchitis and Mother said I had to stay home. 'Please Mummy, can't you wrap me up and take me? Please?' But Mother was taking no chances. My one consolation was that ours would be one of the homes where the group would call in for refreshment.

But really it was no real consolation. For on those nights when we went round singing the well-known carols which I knew off by heart, and would sing with such joy, I think heaven was never closer. The night would be full of stars too, and my imagination would take off. I never understood 'Silent Night' as a child. First we would sing 'Hark the herald angels sing, Glory to the newborn King', so how could the night be silent when so much was happening? But nonetheless those times were all mystery, all wonder, all glory, to me. The lanterns, the music, the singing, Father holding me when I was still very little, and feeling the excitement that was the joy of Christmas. And to miss it! It was terrible! But my *Ayah* was there, and Mother stayed home too this time for I was really very poorly. And later when everyone came they sang for me, so that made things a bit better!

My brothers and I had a Hornby train set, and we added to it with every bit of birthday money we were given. Lighted carriages, signal boxes, lines and lines of track which we laid out, and had so much joy playing with. In Pagoda Road we had so much space, we could lay the lines all the way down the open corridor and just let the engines roll. It was a constant source of joy to us, and when we had to leave Burma when the Japanese invaded we had to leave all our toys and our beloved Hornby behind. We packed it all in a box, and gave it to a Burmese boy whose family were going to stay behind. I know that he would have had as much joy with it as we had had ... But as so many went into concentration camps, I hope this did not happen to him and his family.

It was when we lived at Pagoda Road that I also got mumps. And that just the night before I was be in a dancing display. I was part of a team and we were all to perform in one of the universities. Not a competition or anything like that, but of course I was now out of it. I couldn't have cared less at that moment. My glands were swollen, I was feeling terrible and very sorry for myself, especially as my brothers were not allowed near me. I was alone! I was hoping they would come down with the mumps and then we would all be miserable together, but alas no! They escaped the mumps, and I was very cross about that. But time heals as they say and I got over the mumps and my misery. Later we did a dance with hoops before the Governor General and we had white gauze dresses and silver braid round the waist, and a circlet of flowers round our heads. I was in a seventh heaven. I had not been a bridesmaid at my cousin's wedding, but at last I was dressed in something very pretty and in a way that made up for all the humiliation I suffered then. For the girl who had been the bridesmaid was no dancer so was not chosen for this. And I knew she would have liked to be, and I felt really sorry for her. I even have a picture of myself in my finery, taken on the balcony of the house in Pagoda Road. Short hair, with a fringe and very blonde. I look very pleased. Not proud, just pleased.

While we lived there, the Gobu dam – or was it a reservoir? – was being built, and Father took us there. He knew the man who was in charge of construction and Alan, Tucker and I were very excited. It was so strange walking on the bottom of a place

Author, after dancing at the Town Hall, Burma, 1938.

which would soon be filled with water. Nearby stood an old water tower, and it was another occasion where I nearly died of fright.

The tower was round, and to get to the top one had to climb up winding stairs. These ran on the inside wall of the tower, but did not have railings. Just sort of built into the wall. Looking down all I could see was dark water. Gamely I followed my Father up, and at the top went onto a platform overlooking the whole project. Then going before me, Father said, 'Come along Gracie,' and proceeded to go down leaving me to negotiate the steps on my own. The place was very dim, the steps very wet and slippery for the tower was very old, and I discovered then that I am not very good at heights. I was so afraid that I couldn't speak, and Father had just gone. There was no way that I could walk down, and I was still only seven so my legs were not that long. So I sat on my bottom, and clinging close to the wall I inched my way down. I could imagine what it would be like to fall into that emptiness and end up in the water. I knew I would never survive. So I shut my eyes, asking my guardian angel to stop me from falling and kept on going, just feeling my way. To open my eyes was the last thing I wanted to do, yet to close them was the last thing I should have done. So my angel got me down – not me. I was such a tom-boy and so ready to go where everyone went, and do what everyone did, that it never entered my Father's head that this was a very frightening experience for me. And being me, I finally caught up with him, and never told him. He never did know. But the back of my skirt and my pants were wet from going down on my bottom, and that I had to hide, till they dried. Hot weather has its uses!

It was here that we ended up with a parrot. My eldest sister did anyway. And it bit her! But it was in a sorry condition, so Polly came home with us, and ended his days very happily. He had a cage which hung in a doorway, for he liked to see all that was going on, and it was a doorway that everyone used. So we all said hello each time we passed. He soon learned to say hello back. He could say a lot of other things as well. The legs of his cage were moulded into the floor of the cage and were hollow. At night his cage was covered with a blue lacy cloth – it's funny how little things like that stick in one's mind – and in the morning before it was removed, Polly would have one eye peeping through one of the legs and yelling 'good-morning' till the cloth was removed. We also knew when Father was coming home. How Polly knew five minutes before he arrived that he was due to arrive, we never understood. But the parrot was always right. And he would start screeching, 'Daddy's coming. Daddy's coming.' And sure enough, 'daddy' came. But Polly was not young when we got him, and didn't keep very good health. He had been mistreated and though he was happy and seemed healthy, one day Polly just died. It was terrible. For he collapsed, and then recovered, then collapsed again, and came to, and then finally he collapsed and died. We all wept buckets.

I was chief mourner and undertaker, as I told you earlier, and so Polly's funeral was all a parrot could have hoped for. The best box, the nicest cloth to wrap him in, and of course a song and a prayer. I never could see heaven without animals, and parrots and all beautiful creatures. Not flies and bugs though!

We had our first-ever telephone there also. A big black thing where you took the receiver off the hook and held it, and spoke into a separate mouth piece. Everyone will know about them. It was fixed on the wall, and too high for me to reach, and when the family said, 'Gracie, answer that' I had to get a chair first. I didn't like speaking into it anyway, the receiver was very heavy and I had to use both hands to stop me dropping it. All these lessons I learned as a child I vowed I would never forget when I grew up. And even today, I have found myself pausing, when first I had my children and now grand-children, and before I deal with a situation I try to see it from their perspective. I was afraid of certain things, and so we mustn't assume because we are not, that it would be the same for others. We all react differently to things, and kids won't always tell you for fear of being told, 'Don't be silly'. I hid so much from everyone, and had to fight through fears alone, especially later when I was sent up north to boarding school and was separated from my brothers. More of that later.

The Jubilee Hall was another marvel on that road. It was built to commemorate Queen Victoria's Jubilee and was a magnificent structure. Concerts and theatre and ballet companies came there, and as it was barely a hundred yards from our house, being at the crossroads nearby, we were able to watch all the spectacles. From the outside of course! Each year there would be a huge fair, with giant wheels, and swings and stalls etc. The biggest thrill was the man who dived from a platform very high up into a round tank of water. And before he dived, they would set a ring of fire round the edge of that huge tank. The vast crowd would be silent, and very still. He looked so tiny up there, and I reckon the tank must have looked very small to him down on the ground. I thought he was the bravest man there ever was. Then he would take a deep breath, while all of us held ours, and then he would throw himself off and come hurtling down. Arms straight down, head tucked in, and right into the centre of that tank. Silence, and then it was as if everyone together let their breaths out in a great sigh, and the applause started. And went on and on and on! What a spectacle, what a brave man!

And of course there were the sword swallowers and the nail eaters. But I thought they were stupid, and didn't consider them brave at all. There was one day when I asked my second sister to take me with her and her friend, but I was too small and 'we don't want you tagging along', so I was left behind. About half an hour later they came and said they would take me after all. I was to learn the reason soon enough. A man at a stall was offering a large bottle of 'Balachaung' (I told you about it – Mr Walker used to make it in Insein) – to the first person who could touch the tip of their nose with their tongue. No one could, but my sister knew it was something that was easy for me. An accomplishment that I have never talked about, and certainly today do not go around proving I can do. So I was dragged there. But it was too late. The man had closed the offer as no one had come forward. As I said to them 'See?

If you had taken me in the first place ...'. It does require patience when you are teenager and have a small kid trailing behind.

CHAPTER SIX

Festivals

THE BURMESE WATER FESTIVAL was held in the month of April, and we looked forward to it eagerly and with true delight. The water festival heralded the breaking of the monsoons. April was also the hottest month of the year, so it was a welcome festival.

It may sound like an excuse for the whole nation to behave like children, because young and old alike joined in. But I do assure you, that when clothes stick to your back within five minutes of putting them on with perspiration, and when the only relief comes from sitting under the fans or punkas as they call them out there, and when no amount of water will quench the thirst – then when the first signs of the rainy season appear, any excuse to have a water fight is a very good excuse. We couldn't have our fun in the bathroom during the hot season, for water had to be conserved, so the three days that the water festival lasted was something everyone looked forward to.

First we would prepare our weapons. These were what looked like cycle pumps. But they had a nozzle at the end with either one hole or several and a plunger at the other end. So you could suck the water into the tube and then push it out again. Then we would collect all the containers we could find and keep them ready to fill with water when 'the' day arrived. Mother would get out our oldest clothes, which meant shorts and singlets, and father would cover the bonnet of his car with a waterproof hood. You will soon see the need for this precaution. The moment the first clouds appeared the city would go mad. And for three glorious days everyone would be wetting everyone else. Water fights (happy ones) took place everywhere. Gangs of kids roamed at will with their water cannons. No one escaped, and the streets would be running with water, and people would be dancing and children screaming with delight. One stayed blessedly wet for the three days.

As for us! We had our own private battle with our water pistols. Playing cops and robbers and whatever else our imaginations could conjure up. Poor *Ayah* daren't show her face outside her kitchen. She used to lock and bar the door, only coming out at meal times. But there was a very strict rule, and everyone stuck to it. No water fights within the homes. So we never dared wet *Ayah* even if she came outside, for we valued our food too much.

We kids knew when to draw the line where.

At some time during those three days Father would take us into the city centre. I think all Dad's drivers would be waiting and the car would be stopped again and again and we would all get drenched. We dried in a very short time and so did the car for Father had covered everything he could. The little Burmese and Indian children ran around stark naked, their bodies glistening with water, their faces alight with joy and fun. To be a part of the festival was to simply enjoy it. To enjoy the fun, to accept being wet, to feel the cool water instead of the baking sun and just live for the moment. Even the fire engines used to turn out, and to get caught in their spray was deadly. It was the only time Father would turn the car around and order us to put the windows up. I never heard of anyone getting drowned by one of them, but it was too ferocious a jet of water to get entangled with. Father said they never aimed it at people, just upwards and let the spray fall. But that was enough!

In Insein at Grandma's house, if we were there for the festival we had no less a good time. We had only the well water there, but the well never ran dry anyway. The *mali* (our gardener) used to fill a big barrel. It was five feet deep and as wide, and collected all the rain water also. The poor *mali*! He had to keep it filled for we were not allowed to lean too far over in case we fell in, so we could only take so much water out of it. And of course in Insein we had so much space to run around in, so it wasn't a question of 'You wet me, and I'll wet you' but one of, 'Catch me first.' The rules of the game were simple. Once caught you got wet and vice versa. No one got angry – it was good fun and sporting. My poor cousin was never allowed to join in, nor were some of the other little girls. It wasn't considered ladylike to get wet, and we felt very sorry for them. We knew better than to wet them – not that they would have minded. As for me? I was a little ruffian as my Aunt always called me, and as a result had a wonderful time.

All good things come to an end, for then the rains started in earnest. In Insein of course, with the corrugated roof, it was deafening, even though the huge trees surrounding the house gave some shelter. In my own self's house, the tennis court would be covered in water, and if there was no lightning or thunder, then Mother would let us go out and play in the rain. We would spend a couple of glorious hours doing just that. Victor and Freddie were with us, and we would charge around having a great time! When my kids were small there was a time when we had a very large garden, and people thought I was mad because if there was a heavy downpour, I would put their swimming costumes on and send them out to play in the rain. 'They'll catch their death of cold' – but they never did. More parents should let their kids out to play in the rain in summer time. Good for the skin!

Then of course there was the Light Festival. That was in October. I have no idea what this was in aid of, and I'm sure anyone reading this and who knows can answer this question, but for me as a child it was enough that this festival happened. It was very colourful and lovely. Most houses would be decorated with Chinese lanterns on the outside. Whole strings of them outlining the houses and the gateways. Some would have huge stars made of paper and lit from the inside, outside their front doors. There were shapes of all kinds and in all colours. Dragons, snakes, stars, balls, crescents, crosses and so many others. Some very large, some small, but all beautiful. The whole of Rangoon lit up. Father would take us out when it was dark, all of us wrapped in blankets for in October it was chilly in the evenings, and he would drive slowly through the centre of town and the suburbs so we could see the decorations. Rangoon was like a gigantic Christmas tree lit up. Every house had different shapes and colours. Even the smallest and poorest areas had put up lights of some kind. And of course most of them were lit by candles inside. There was never any news of fire from them. These Chinese lanterns were very well made, and so were the other shapes. Great care was taken. The effect on us as children was wonderland. I remember wanting to hold the colours and the light in my hand which sounds foolish. But there was a part of me that wanted to hold onto that colour and light and reflected beauty and never let it go. How I miss those moments in my life! How I remember the Burma that was, with such an ache of longing. Do they still have the water festival, the light festival? They were traditions, so I suppose they do. We all have fleeting moments in our lives when something touches us so deeply that the mind retains the memory of it. So my memory remembers the boisterous occasion of the Water Festival, and the gentle beauty of the Light Festival.

Although this is not about a festival, it has to do with father taking us out at night to see things. We never knew when it would happen! He would never promise to take us here or there in case work prevented him from doing so and he hated breaking a promise. What he did was far better! He would come home and say to Mother, 'Girlie, get the children out of bed and let's go out!' 'Out' could be anywhere! It could mean going to Mogul Street where the Indian restaurants were, or to China Town, or to Insein, or for a trip round the lakes to see the moon rise. Whereever he took us was a thrill! An exciting, cosy and warm feeling would flood through us and we three were content. My dear Father – Daddy – who was so loving and kind. And trusting!

Mogul Street was terrific! The Muslims and Hindus had their food stalls and restaurants there. All the fronts were open, and charcoal burners resided on the pavements, and kebabs spluttered on them and sent out delicious mouth-watering smells.

Chapattis, and *paratas* and hot meat and potato balls, and the aroma of meat, vegetable and other curries came wafting through the car windows. 'Please stop Daddy?' And of course he did. Stormkings – spirit pressure lamps – sent out a powerful white light, which mixed with the red of the fires, and the hot brown faces of the cooks. And shone on the patient waiting faces of the eaters. Like us! For that was one of the treats my father often gave us. Sitting in the car, with the door open, while Dad talked to all his friends. Everyone knew him and there we would sit while he ordered food for us. We would watch as it was cooked and we too would share in the warmth and friendship around us. At last it would be ready. Oh the taste of the meat and potato balls and the *samosas* and whatever else was given to us. Hard to describe except to say that Indian food cooked like that, fresh and smelling of charcoal – kebabs never taste the same done any other way – was something that even today brings back a yearning to eat the way Indian food should be eaten. With our fingers, and licking them to death afterwards so as not to miss any lingering taste – that's the way to do it!

Then having been stuffed to the brim, father would head for home, but us three would fall asleep. And we would be transferred still sleeping soundly, to our beds, waking up the next morning and wondering if it had all been a beautiful dream.

China Town was the same in some ways but more organized. None of the bustling chaos of Mogul Street, though one could eat at tables on the side of the road. For the food was cooked indoors. But it was still a thrill for us. Even here everyone knew Father – being the MTO brought him into contact with so many, and it was always nice to be welcomed because of him. The Burmese and the Chinese, once you have made a friend of them, remain friends always. We made many friends all our lives there, and never lost them. The war changed much, but friendships like that can be treasured forever. Two of my closest pals were Burmese, but we were separated in the war and later I was not able to trace their whereabouts. But on these excursions we had to wait while all the polite exchanges were made. How are all your family? And how are all yours? Is your Mother well? Yes, and yours? And so on and so forth. This was the polite thing to do first – then friendship and everyday chat would take over. What we loved too was the way children play such a part in their lives. It isn't a question of children being seen and not heard. They are respected, and treated as persons in their own right. And young as they are, the older ones will happily take care of the littler ones and be very responsible towards them. Perhaps I was seeing things in a way grown-ups didn't see them. Perhaps too, things were not as I saw them? I don't know. I am speaking of my childhood memories, and these were the things that spoke to me. And my brothers too! It wasn't the same in the homes of the richer people for they seemed to behave in a way that reflected life as we lived it. But the ordinary Burmese and Indians, who though poorer, had a dignity that even as a child I seemed to see. And respect. Because they respected their children, and their elderly parents and relations. I thought them free, and sometimes envied the children for they seemed to be so happy. I wasn't sure even then that having money and clothes and education was the way to freedom! I do know that when their parents asked them to do something, they asked politely and the children would just happily do it to oblige their honourable parent. Alan, Tucker and I mixed with a lot of these kids. When we played on the big open spaces – *midarns* they were called – we would have a lot of these kids watching us when we played rounders, and we would include them and get to know them. I don't think my parents ever knew how many I used to talk and play with. My Father was like that too. All men were equal to him, and he treated everyone with respect, one reason his drivers loved him. He taught me to be the same, and I shall always be grateful for his leading. He didn't preach Jesus – he lived Jesus.

Talking about food makes me think of mangoes. Grandma had many mango trees in Insein. And we had a mango season too. When the mangoes began to ripen we would go to Grandma's house and make ourselves sick eating them. Grandma knew that to stop us would be useless, but to let us get sick of them would teach us prudence. The hard way! But they were juicy and beautiful, and with a huge bowl full of them, the temptation was hard to resist. After the first stuffing, so to speak, we would slow down. But oh! Those mangoes. I don't know what was done with the hundreds that came from the trees, or the guavas or the Jackfruit. For we certainly couldn't get through all the fruit there was. Of course Mr Walker had a hand in all this, with his mango pickle and chutney. But mango pickle isn't made with ripe mangoes, so he took his from the tree before the ripening. Magical times. Unfortunately some people suffered from mango boils which were horrible. But none of us kids did.

Papayas were lovely too. Pawpaws they are called in some countries. We had a tree in Malagong, and the leaves of the tree spread large and wide. The one we had was near the kitchen which stood about five yards apart from the house with a covered way leading to it. Puck, our beloved cat who died in a war with another cat which I told you about, used to walk from the back veranda to the kitchen roof, and one day thought the leaves of the papaya tree was an extension of the roof and stepped onto it. Cats always land on their feet, and this proved it. He fell – onto his feet – shook his head in disbelief, and never did it again. He was fine, though visibly shaken. Our papayas were large and juicy. The ones I see today are miserable specimens to the ones we had then.

And then there were the custard apples. How to describe them? They had a soft skin which was rather like an overstuffed quilt, with bumps. Easy to break open, they were the size of a large orange. Inside the fruit was white. Little oval pods with black seeds which were soft and 'custardy'. We ate them with a teaspoon, and us kids kept the seeds and made bean bags out of them. Better than a ball at times, they were great to throw around, and made a nice sound too. I miss all those wonderful fruits which grew around us. Jackfruit which grew on the trunk of the tree. Great heavy fruit with a hedgehog outer skin, cut short. Yellow pods of fruit, laid out in rows. Chewy and lovely to eat. You needed a chopper to open the fruit, the outer skin was so tough. And then there was the bale fruit, which I have never heard of since. We had a tree in Pagoda Road, and when the bale fruit were ready, they would fall. As their skins were as hard as rock, no one was allowed to use that driveway till they were all down. The trees were huge, so it was not possible just to climb and get them. They could crack open a person's skull, and we were all aware of the danger. Children take for granted the things they grow up with, and we were no different in that respect. But I do know that I was very lucky to have my brothers and parents and sisters, and a Grandma who was so special. I do remember feeling safe. My own fears, and hopes and dreams were something they knew nothing about. But that was not their fault. Even today I seem open and friendly – outgoing I am told – yet in me there are things I would never let anyone know about. All humans are like that I know, but some people can talk about all kinds of things. I cannot. And I would always stay away from some people. There was something in them I instinctively distrusted, and I kept my distance. Even as a child, and at times Mother would get angry with me. 'What's wrong with you? Come and say hello.' I would go, and get kissed and hate it. There was one such person who visited Grandma, and he always had a rough chin. And I dreaded his visits, because he would pick me up and rub his chin against my face, and it terrified me.

I used to go and hide when he came, but my Aunt always found me, and I would have to go through the whole thing. I suppose he was just being friendly to a small child, and being playful, but to me? I never said anything, for he was a well-thought of man, and who was I, a child to say I didn't like him?

I've got off the track. Started with festivals, went onto food, then fruit and now my likes and dislikes. Sorry!

CHAPTER SEVEN

Thandoung

THANDOUNG WAS A HILL STATION where we went on holiday. It was north of Rangoon and not far from a place called Toungoo. Father would drive us all up there and then go back to Rangoon to work.

We rented a bungalow on a hill from a lady doctor who lived just below. Not a big hill, for there were steps cut into the side – deep and wide – for us to reach the bungalow, made with gravel because of the rains, and wood propping up each step. We used to leap down them, and one day I slipped and took all the skin off my thighs, which hurt terribly. Iodine made it even worse, but any germs lurking around were killed off at once. The bungalow was on wooden posts about three feet off the ground, again because of rain, and snakes and other animals. Thandoung was a bit wild, and we always had to be careful. Our *Ayah* used to come with us, but one year her daughter Rungamar came instead. She must have only been about eighteen, but when you are only six, eighteen is old. No electric lights or running water and we didn't mind that at all. The nights were like Grandma's house when we sat around a table playing cards and other games.

We had the odd tiger and panther coming down from the higher hills, but Thandoung itself was a hill station. Winding earth roads, with deep valleys and precipices to one side and forest on the other. In the crevices and hollows acorns grew and orchids. So very beautiful, but we never picked them. It was nicer just to look and leave them there. It was wild and beautiful, dangerous and exciting. Most days we would go for walks, which would last anything from one hour to four, depending on where we went. The seven-mile stream was a favourite place. Huge boulders with the water rushing around them, fed by a waterfall a bit further up. One day we were nearly there when one of the villagers told us to turn back. A tiger had stolen a calf, and had taken it down to the stream. But it hadn't finished the carcass and would come back later, so they advised us to leave the area as fast as we could. I couldn't keep up with the fast pace the grown-ups set, so one of our party carried me piggy back. It was a strange feeling really, for on both sides of the seven-mile stream we walked through forest, with clear patches in between and I was expecting the tiger to come charging at us at any moment. But John who was carrying me on his shoulders assured us kids that the tiger was probably sleeping after its meal. No consolation at all, especially as Father wasn't there with his revolver.

Very often friends came and joined us, and John was one of them We all loved him and he was good fun. We knew the whole family, for they were one of the families who lived on the estate in Malagong. So he was a part of us also and remained so as long as he lived which was a long time.

Poor Rungamar! The kitchen overlooked the winding road below our hill, and outside the kitchen window stood the chicken hut, its corrugated roof on a level with the windowsill. There were many wild cats around, and normally they did not bother us, but at times hunger would bring them right up to the house to try and get to the chickens. One day one leapt onto the roof of the hut and glared at Rungamar and she screamed her head off.

We thought she was being attacked, but she was not used to this primitive life, and was very scared. Alas that cat would not go away, and they can be quite vicious; also they can be very large, as this one was. And it kept us in the house. At night it kept jumping onto the roof trying to find a way in, so Father decided he had to scare it off. He didn't want to kill it! So he waited and when it came close enough he fired near it and it got the message and took off. Rungamar never came with us again, she was too scared.

The Karens, who are a lovely people, ran the vegetable gardens in Thandoung. This was quite a walk away, but we would go shopping there. Artesian wells were sunk throughout the gardens, and the vegetables were wonderful. I have never seen such large tomatoes, they were as big as my Father's open hand, and were firm and delicious. The Karens always gave me one to eat. This place was the source of the food for the people who lived in the hills around, and for those few residents like the doctor who lived up there. They would also come around to the bungalow with long narrow baskets which they carried on their backs, and which were suspended from a wide headband. If you have ever seen the Sherpas in the Himalyas carrying their loads you will know what I mean. In these baskets would be bananas, and wild honey, and Mother always bought from them.

There were tea plantations up there also, and when the tea had been plucked the bushes were burnt, and we would watch the fires from the house. It was like watching a river of fire running swiftly. The fires would start from one end, and then race up and down the rows of bushes till all was burnt. Then planting started again. I don't know the ins and outs of tea growing or even why they burnt these bushes, but burn them they did and that's all I knew.

Night was full of noises up there. Hyenas calling to each other, barking deer calling to each other, the cry of strange birds, and often the roar of a large animal who had ventured close to where humans were. I was too small to remember the time a tiger rubbed itself against the walls of the house, purring contentedly. Mother says it was frightening because the latch on the front door wasn't very strong and they had to put furniture against it in case the tiger tried to come in.

Then there was the time I nearly got blood poisoning. And all my own fault! I hated shoes – still do – and would go barefoot as often as I could. Playing outside the house while Mother had gone to the vegetable gardens, I stood on a plank of wood which had a rusty nail in it, and it sank right into the sole of my left heel. Really deep. I washed it, didn't tell *Ayah*, nor did I tell Mother when she came home. The evening passed and I began to feel ill, and my heel throbbed. I was only about five and a half then. Bedtime and I began to burn up and toss and turn and then murmur to myself – I was half-way to delirium by then. It awoke Mother and she called *Ayah* and I remember her saying 'Where does it hurt?' and finally pointing to my foot I said no more. They were horrified at what they saw. The whole heel underneath was full of pus with a black ring in the middle and a nasty red line going up my foot. No telephone, no hospital, no car for Father was away. *Ayah* put the kettle on the stove which was always hot, and Mother got out the Epsom salts, and they started to put hot compresses on it. They worked into the early hours of the morning with Mother praying that I wouldn't die, and finally the whole heel exploded. It was like a dam bursting. The towel that was underneath my foot just took the terrible pus and green and black stuff that came out, and the relief for me was something I will never forget. The fever and the pain and my foggy brain just cleared. And the red line receded. I didn't know then how very close I was to blood poisoning. But I still keep Epsom salts around. Hot fomentations of that will draw anything out! Like my scalded back, I didn't say anything and nearly died. But I always got scolded when things like that happened, and I didn't realize why till I as a parent myself would be cross with my kids, not because they had done something wrong, but that they could have seriously hurt themselves and I reacted to that. Love can do that to a person I guess.

Then there were the different rock formations. Slipper rock: which really did look like a gigantic slipper. But the walk to get to this rock was on a narrow path with a drop on one side. Also it was very damp and slippery there and water used to trickle down the sides of the rock and on the inside of the slipper. Added to which leeches used to be in abundance there. The damp I suppose. I hated them. My brother Alan seemed to be the one to whom they attached themselves and they really cling to the skin once they get a hold, and he used to shudder. Salt will get them off, but we didn't always carry salt with us. I had the odd one, and I would just stand while someone got the thing loose. They are funny things, yet saved my Father's life years and years later, when he came out of Burma. Thousands had to walk out through jungle and rivers and swamps to escape the Japanese, and he got a poisoned leg. So he put leeches on it, and they sucked out the poison and kept his leg clean. So they have uses, but to us as kids they were – ugh!

The other rock was elephant rock. This one was huge and balanced on the edge of one of the roads overlooking the hills surrounding Thandoung. It really did resemble an elephant, but we were never allowed to climb it because it was near the edge of a sheer drop. Remarkable formation! It was almost as though a giant hand had carved it, and perhaps it had! God has created a marvellous world for us and we don't always appreciate it!

Holiday time for us in Thandoung was very special. The picnics we went on, when we ate off banana leaves, for they make excellent plates; the walks, the danger too, which we were all aware of, yet knowing that animals are shy of humans and will not attack unless defending their young, or are very hungry. Trusting too the grown-ups who were with us, for we never went out alone, it would have been too risky. Getting car-sick on the way down to Toungoo, because of the hairpin bends, and wishing I was anywhere but in the car, but getting over it eventually. The seven-mile stream which was wonderful for swimming – I was never allowed in, it was too deep, but I used to dangle my legs in it. I have a photograph taken on one of the boulders, and realize how very small we three were. I do remember the picture being taken. All three of us flaxen-haired!

One night there was a tremendous storm, with lightning and thunder, and a thunderbolt too. The next morning I picked up a piece of rock outside the bungalow and showed it to Father, who showed it to a friend. They said it was part of a meteorite which had hit, and what we had thought was a thunderbolt. Pieces were scattered all over, but I kept this one till we left Burma. It was very strange looking, and had stripes of colour in it, and was obviously broken off from a larger piece. There was no other rock like it in Thandoung, so I suppose it did come from above.

Father knew Thandoung well, and as a young man went up there quite a lot. He was also a very good shot. When once they had a man-eating tiger roaming around and killing flocks, and it had killed a villager, so they asked Father to kill it. He built a machan – which is a platform in a tree camouflaged with branches – and spent the night there. A goat was tied to the bottom of the tree to act as bait. But nothing happened then, and it was just as well. For Father, testing the gun out on another target, discovered that the bullets were duds. If the tiger had come, the goat and probably father as well would have perished. He went back to Rangoon and got another box of bullets and returned to Thandoung. This time the tiger did come and was killed. What the outcome of the dud bullets was I was never told. My Father never killed for the sake of killing, or for game. He loved animals and he loved the beauty of the big cats. Snakes when they were a real threat to lives, as were the cobras in Malagong, were something else. He taught my brothers and me to shoot also, with a rifle and with a revolver. And we were all good shots, and respected guns. Alan as a young man used to shoot at Bisley here in England many years later when he was with the RAF after the war. But then my father taught us so much. He taught us about cars, for he was a mechanical engineer, he taught us carpentry, and so much else. He taught us to be careful of things, to be aware of others, to be respectful of our elders and to be kind to everyone, never making distinctions between race and colour, rich or poor. My Father was a tremendous man! When I was very small he would take me on his knee and call me Grace Wynne. Especially when he knew I had a bad day, or had been in some kind of trouble. Like the time when I was barely two, and Victor's eldest sister was having her eighteenth birthday. Victor and I were allowed to stay up late, and we were sitting on the back of a sofa, and we started to rock it. It tipped over backwards and Victor and I banged our heads. I don't think I got the blame for that! But I was taken home by my *Ayah* who was very cross, but not with me, so perhaps I was blamed for it after all! Victor was the only boy and he had many sisters who all spoilt him. He toughened up when he joined us. But on this day, I was very upset and it was my Dad who placed me on his knee and made everything right.

Thandoung also had its own 'mountain'; Thandounggyi it was called. And every so often an excursion was made up it. I used to climb trees like a cat and shin up almost anything, but when it came to heights like that I was a very unhappy little girl, especially as everyone left me to follow on. It was all right going up, but coming down was awful. I was afraid I would start to slip and there would be no stopping. Here again I told no one. It was the same as in the water tower – I was terrified there and I was always afraid here. Never afraid of pain, but the way down looked so far to my young eyes. In reality it was really just a very large hill, I think. But as far as I was concerned it was Everest. My brothers were fine with it, and would leave me far behind, every so often someone shouting, 'Come along Gracie, don't be so slow'. How were they to know when I never told them? Another lesson I vowed I would never forget!

It was in Thandoung that I got bitten by an Alsatian. It belonged to the lady doctor, and was a lovely dog. But one day I was running with a stick and the dog thought I was going to hit it, so it bit me on the calf of my right leg. It wasn't a deep bite, though I still carry the scar, but it hurt, and the poor dog was very sorry. He kept licking me afterwards. My *Ayah* was alone with us kids and she did something I have never ever heard of. After putting the inevitable iodine on the bite, she placed a copper one pice piece on it. The pain just went, just like that! And the bite healed very quickly. The dog was not rabid, so I was spared the injections. He and I were good friends after that, but I learned that dogs react to a stick, unless one is throwing it for them.

We all loved Thandoung, and Father bought some land up there to build a house. The land was on a plateau on a hill and had lovely views. We used to go up there and pick wild raspberries. There was an old ruin of a house there and Father was going to build round it. But war broke out, and of course we never returned to Burma – not as a family to live, that is. So the land is still there, probably very overgrown, but lost to us. We all had dreams and plans over it, and because we all loved Thandoung it was something so special. Tucker, Alan and I didn't talk about it ever – I think we each felt the pain because the memories were so good. We each have our own remembrances, and it may be that they are at fault in many ways. I just remember things as they appeared to me, and that is all I can go by. Each place has a special place in my heart – and sometimes to be told, 'it wasn't like that at all' could be true, but how each of us as children see things should never be destroyed. Sometimes children have a clearer vision than older people for nothing is cluttered up. My brothers and I found life very clear-cut and simple. We relied on instinct and childish logic, which is not a bad thing. That we survived the dangers that we faced in so many different ways was due to the love and security we had within the family itself.

We loved Thandoung, and the red bungalow – for that was its colour – and we loved the Karens up there, and the wildness, and the beauty, and the wonder of just being alive!

CHAPTER EIGHT

Maymyo

IN 1939, BEFORE MY NINTH BIRTHDAY, my Father's job was to send him up North to Lashio. This meant that Mother would go also, and our time in Rangoon, and Insein, and Thandoung was to come to an end. Suddenly, this part of my childhood, which I thought would never end, was over. And I was the first one to be sent away. Both my sisters were in University, so they could have rooms there. And they were together. But I was to go to boarding school and leave my brothers behind. For the first time in my life I was to be without anyone and sent to a place two days and a night away, and do the journey on my own.

The preparations were made. I was to go to a school called St Michael's which my Mother had attended as a girl. I was bought a tin trunk which was a shiny yellow and had flowers painted on it. Inside was the new school uniform. Six of everything. Six shirts, white and crisp, six skirts – I think the colour was blue and why I can't remember that I do not know. A school blazer, six pairs of knickers, (they were not called panties then, so I call them by their old name), six pairs of white socks, six handkerchiefs, six vests (cotton of course) – towels, facecloths (2), gym shoes, black leather shoes, the ones with a strap and a buckle, two pairs of shorts for gym. And all the other things like pyjamas, a jumper, toothbrush and toothpaste etc. Everything packed beautifully into my little yellow trunk. And of course two or three dresses for the weekends. And if I remember rightly we wore school uniform to church. All was ready.

I lived in a state of numbness at that time. I wanted to pinch

St Michael's Chapel.

myself and wake up and find it was all a dream gone horribly wrong. But no, the nightmare was real. Goodbyes had to be said. Going to Grandma's house to say goodbye to her and Mr Walker and the *mali* and *Ayah*. And Grandma saying, 'Time will soon pass and you will be back here before you know where you are.' And knowing somehow that this would never be. In fact I was to see Insein only once more briefly. But being me, I didn't cry. No one was going to see how afraid I was, and already lonely. Once more to Malagong, and to see my own self's house for what I thought was to be the last time. But I did see it once more when war broke out and we returned to Rangoon to fetch my sisters. After that I never saw it again – and I grieve for it even today. I even dream that I am back looking for it, and even in my dreams I never find it. Is it still there? Or lost in the bombing, or burnt down? I shall never know. There is a compartment in my heart even today that is separate from all other occasions and times, and I made that compartment at that tender age. How did I know it was the beginning of a time in my life that would never be repeated?

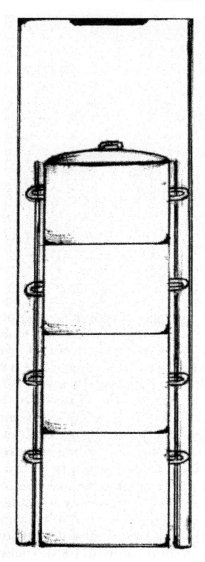

Tiffin carrier.

Never! But I knew. My Mother called it the beginning of my independence, when I decided that I stood alone and had to cope the best I knew how. She often found fault with me over it, but I had never been separated from my brothers – they were two solid rocks for me – and now they were taken from me. I had an abounding faith in Jesus, and my guardian angel. It may sound foolish to most, but I knew they were there. Yet, even as I cried to Him and said 'I know You are there', still physically I was alone. I know He understood, even at that age, and I was allowed to grieve over what I was losing. My problem was I wouldn't let anyone see my pain.

The day I left for Maymyo, was, cruelly, the first day of the Water Festival. There were other girls on that train going to the school and someone called Kitty was to look after me, but no one came near me till I was at the other end. My parents and my brothers came to see me off. I was in a second class compartment which had wooden seats. My yellow trunk was put in, and my bedroll. It had a soft something or other to sleep on and a blanket and a pillow – a bit like the old Wild West I often thought. It was in a roll with a strap around it. I also had a tiffin carrier. These were four aluminium containers which had loops each side, and fitted into each other. Then the four were held together by an oblong handle which had loops also which slid through the loops on the sides of the containers. Hard to describe! In this was my food for the two days and night I would be travelling. My *Ayah* had put in all the things I like. Rice in the bottom with a chapatti. The next had chicken curry with a small jar of mango pickle. The second to the top had two meat cutlets and potato and onion balls, and *samosas*, and was packed with bits and pieces she had added. The top container had some Indian sweetmeats, an apple, a mango, bread and butter in greaseproof paper, some Chinese dried fruit, and a piece of cheese. Also a spoon and fork and a cloth. I must have had water in a bottle or something, but I don't remember that for some reason. So I would be well fed even if I was miserable. Unfortunately I was so miserable that I ate all the food within the first two hours, and spent the rest of the journey with an aching and finally empty tummy. It was the longest and saddest journey I have ever taken. I love trains, I love the countryside, and Burma is so beautiful, but I was wrapped up in a cloud of longing for all I was leaving behind and it seemed the end of the world to me.

I perked up a bit when we reached Mandalay, and started the climb up to Maymyo. The train had to zig-zag up. Forward, then back onto another track, then forward again. All familiar to me having spent hours watching the trains at my Uncle Tom's house, shunting back and forth. It was a long slow grind, till we reached level ground, and finally steamed into Maymyo. It was there that the other girls who I had not seen at all tumbled out of the train and someone said was there someone called Gracie something or other around. I was very much around, apprehensive and lost. So here was a lifeline! We all got into some jut-carts and headed for the school. A jut-cart which is what we called a covered *tonga* on wheels, and pulled by a horse. I always enjoyed going in them, better than a rickshaw. In a rickshaw I always felt sorry for the man who pulled it, but with a horse I felt a lot better. Talking about rickshaws brings to my mind the thin yet strong legs of those men. Bulging with

St Michael's School, Maymyo.

effort with the veins standing out. Knowing better now, I think they were varicose veins, and what those men had to pull at times it's no wonder! ... But here I was on the way to St Michael's School ...

My first impression was one of warmth. Unlike our bricks and mortar school in Rangoon, St Michael's was a rambling wooden construction, more like a country house than a school. It had a huge porch in front, and the windows were large and friendly with curtains. There were trees all around, and the drive curved in a semi-circle with large wooden gates. My spirits began to perk up. This was more like Grandma's house and my own self's house rolled together. I was ushered in, and realized that actually we had arrived a day earlier than most of the others, so the place wasn't teeming with pupils. Then I had my first shock! We were met at the entrance by a tall imposing figure in a nun's habit. She was the head of the school, Sister Harriet. I did not know that nuns ran a Protestant school. But so they did, and there was nothing in our teaching or worship that was Roman Catholic in any way, for they were indeed Protestants themselves. So we had four Sisters who were also teachers. Sister Harriet, Sister Lettuce, Sister Elsie and Sister Louis who was very old and didn't show herself too often.

So here I was facing this imposing figure who looked very stern. Then she spoke and the sun came out. 'Come here my child and welcome to the school.' And she kissed me on both cheeks. Well! That was a good start! 'Now Kitty' (this to the girl who had me in tow) 'take Gracie up to her dormitory, Matron is up there and will show her where she is to sleep. Then come down again and I will show you round the school Grace. Don't worry about your luggage, Matron will see to that.' So up I went. Wide wooden stairs led from the downstairs hall, then a landing and a second flight – memories of Malagong and my first excursion down stairs very similar to these ones flooded in. At the top was a huge landing. On either side were two large dormitories, and in front and over the porch, was also a room with windows all around in which were six beds. Not where I was to go, though later I did sleep there. I was in the first bed on the left as we turned into the right hand dormitory. All the beds had mosquito nets, but these were pulled back neatly to the head of the bed and had a blue sash around each one. At night all we did was pulled them forward for they were on runners. I always found mosquito nets cosy, and this was the first thing I noticed. The dormitories themselves were warm and had big windows with shutters; the whole effect was one of warmth, light and cosiness. Our clothes were kept in lockers in a separate room and Matron had charge of this. All I remember was that each day my school clothes were put out for me, and at the weekend I had a choice of which dress I would wear.

When I had met Matron and she had taken charge of my luggage, Kitty took me down again and we met up with Sister Harriet again. It was then that I was introduced to the other Sisters. Sister Elsie – Luddoo we called her and I don't know why – showed me around. She was a lovely lady, and we became good friends, especially as I used to go walkabout. Having had such a free upbringing, suddenly the confines of the school grounds were more than I could bear. So when I felt like getting out I just went. That one wasn't supposed to do that at boarding school didn't occur to me. I would just walk out and take a look at the world in general and then return. I never missed class, or study time. I just went in our free times. Later I was to learn that they had got in touch with my parents, and apparently Mother had said not to worry. It was against the rules, but as there was not anything anyone could do, Sister Elsie came to me and said she too liked going for walks and so every time I felt like a walk just to let her know and she would come with me. And so she did, and I think I shared more with her than I ever had with anyone before. Actually we were taken for walks as a school. Most days the 'crocodile' of girls would go out in twos and round the block so to speak. Maymyo was a hill station, but quite large nonetheless, so we would walk through roads where houses had huge gardens, and then there would be open spaces. But even then it wasn't the same as going for a walk on one's own and investigating the surrounding area.

The day after we arrived, the other boarders started to turn up. Cars and jut-carts kept coming and going all day, and soon the school was filled with kids my age, and older girls too. I was one of a handful of newcomers, so still not sure of everything, and feeling a bit lost. And suddenly missing my brothers and so retreating into my own corner once again. For a very friendly and open child, I could sometimes be totally unapproachable, and locked into a world of my own. I hadn't realized that at times I seemed formidable even at that age. It was many years later when I was directing a play, that someone said to me, 'Wow, no one would dare to approach you when you are in one of your contemplative moments, they'd be too scared'. That shook me, because that was not so. But that I gave that impression made me reassess the way it must look to others. It was only that I needed to get into my own mind and sort out the things that were going through it at the time which gave that impression. Oh dear! How do children tell even their own parents that they need time to themselves?

But as the day wore on and then during the evening meal, I began to thaw out. And the other girls were very nice and friendly and began to show me the ropes. The next day classes were to start, and so it was early to bed, but not before we all had to go to chapel. How I loved it! It was at the end of one long corridor. All of us had to put veils over our heads. These were triangular squares of white cloth which tied under our hair at the back. Made us all look like angels, which most of us most definitely were not. But we would file into the chapel and sit quietly. One of the Sisters would read a lesson, and then we would sing a psalm and I loved the tunes. And of course there were the old favourites that we would sing, and these I knew well. Then a prayer was said and we would all go out. On most school days this took place after the evening study period, followed by supper and a bit of relaxation time then bed. The school had electric light of course, but once we were all in bed, with our mosquito nets tucked in, one of the Sisters or mostly Matron would come around with a lantern going past each bed slowly to make sure everyone was OK. At which point all whispering would cease till she had departed. Bedtime is something I have always looked forward to. Not because I was tired, but because it meant a time of sharing and giggling with my brothers, and in Insein playing our games in the big four-poster. Here at St Michael's, it was little girls all whispering and sharing things in the dark which would never be shared in the daylight. I think we all got to know each other better at bedtime then at any other time.

I wish I could remember where the toilet was. I have completely forgotten where it was situated – but it had to be somewhere I suppose. I do remember that the daytime toilets and the bath house were in a separate building. It was a large corrugated hut, and divided into lots of cubicles with showers. And of course the daily ritual of bathtime was imposed here also. Nothing had changed in that direction.

Church on a Sunday: I was used to the type of worship we had in our church in Rangoon and now had to get used to what I realize now was rather High Church. We had to make a little dip towards the altar when we went in and on the way out. Then the prayers went on for ever. All read from a book, and each Sunday it seemed we said the same things over and over again. Sometimes it varied but not much. And we had to remain on our knees the whole time. If I had not known Jesus from a child in the way that I did, with the simple truth of the gospel as I learned it from my parents, this would not have helped my spiritual life in any way. It seemed to have nothing to do with God at all. It was ritual and repetition and rather cold and empty. It didn't raise my spirit to high heaven as it used to in Rangoon especially when Mr Gaddis the evangelist came. And what astonished me was the fact that the priests didn't know any of it by heart. As far as I could see from my childish perspective, as they said the same words every week why did they still have to read them? So though the church was a large imposing building I decided that God didn't live there. He couldn't possibly. Not in those cold surroundings, where quite a few little girls didn't understand much of what was happening, and whose knees each week suffered agonies. I did notice that many grown-ups didn't stay on their knees, but we had to and to sit up was to be told 'Kneel!' by one of the prefects in charge of us little ones. No! Sunday morning and church were not on my list of things I liked doing. And it was a shame, and is a shame when ritual can stifle so much that God wants us to receive from Him. But I still had Jesus, and I still had my guardian angel, though I rather fancied that both stayed outside till after the service was over. The rest of Sunday after we had lunch was fairly relaxed, though we did have to have an hour on our beds after lunch, to read or whatever.

Then quite suddenly things changed. My brothers were sent up to a boys' school nearby. What joy! I was to see them again. And I did, though very rarely, but at least they were not far away and that made all the difference to me. And then again, suddenly things took a different turning. My Mother decided to take a house in Maymyo and we would be day scholars for a while.

The house she rented was a bungalow on Nestwood Hill, behind the school but up a long steep hill. It was about three feet off the ground on stilts, and was very nice. It had a curved

Maymyo, 'Nestwood Hill'.

drive, lined with eucalyptus trees and a flower bed which also went all the way round with gladioli. We were together again, my brothers and I, and I have a picture of us taken there, one of the few photos salvaged from the war. We three look very pleased with ourselves. And my *Ayah* came up also! And that was an added joy and blessing. But alas, this was not to last! My Mother felt something was wrong with the house. It had an atmosphere which made her ill at ease and uncomfortable. My *Ayah* also felt the same and finally had to return to Rangoon. I felt no ill-feeling from the house at all, yet Mother took ill there, Alan was very ill there, the kitten nearly died, and my sister came to visit and she got very ill also. And no one knew what with. Tucker and I seemed immune. So finally although Mother had taken a lease on the house, she put us back as boarders and closed the place up. But I still went walkabout, and so used to go to the house and spend time there and eat the plums off the trees. I never understood what it was at the time, but later we learned that the place had a very sad history. I never felt the sadness there, maybe because my guardian angel walked with me wherever I went. Don't laugh! Angels exist, and there are many thousands in this world today who will tell you so.

But we were back at school, and Mother returned to Lashio to be with Father. So that was that, and we three had to make the best of it.

When holiday time came, we did not return to Rangoon, but stayed instead at a hostel not far from the railway station. A very homely and pleasant place, and we used to have a nice time there. Tucker and I had saved our pocket money and rented two bikes. We called them Bullet and Spitfire and careered around Maymyo on them pretending to be dive bombers one moment, and racing drivers the next. I think we scared quite a few people the way we madly dashed around. Why Alan was not included in this I do not remember. But Mother also had a cycle and on one of our more sedate evening rides with her for some reason she came off her bike and broke her wrist. I really don't know how it happened because we were not fooling around. I think she thought it was our fault, but I don't think it was because we were on our best behaviour. So that was the end of that!

Time went on and school was OK. I used to watch the seniors play basketball and vowed that one day I would also. That I did eventually do so, was just another dream that came true. I loved all sport, but was still prone to bronchitis attacks which held me back. But one day, I said to myself, one day I will. And one day I did. But it was not now, not at this time. I could still only dream and keep those dreams to myself. Though I still did recitations and was once in the school concert where I recited and acted out a short poem ... I still remember it though I do not know who wrote it:

> I saw him at work one day, in a castle ditch
> Where foxgloves grow.
> A wrinkled, wizened and bearded elf
> Spectacles stuck on his pointed nose.
> Leather apron, shoe in his hand.
> 'Rip-rap, tip-tap, tip tap too
> A butterfly on my hat, away the moth flew.
> Buskins for a fairy prince, brogues for his son
> Pay me well, pay me well when the job is done.'

> The rogue was mine, beyond a doubt
> I stared at him, he stared at me!
> He pulled a snuff box out.
> Offered the box with a whimsical grace
> 'Poof' he flung the stuff in my face
> And while I sneezed, 'Atishoo' – was gone.

I can remember that I did it on my own, and I am not quite sure how it worked out, but I remember having to do it twice. That was my only chance at doing anything at St Michael's. Still, the future lay ahead, and it wasn't the future we dreamed about.

For the Japanese bombed Pearl Harbour, and started their invasions of all the land around us, and finally Burma itself.

Our school was chosen to be headquarters for the Army, and we were all to be sent home. It was with great sadness that we began to pack all our things together. There was a feeling of the unexpected, for we kids didn't really know what was happening in the world. Up to now, the war had been taking place the other side of the world, and now the enemy was at our door. As yet Rangoon had not been bombed, or invaded, but the grown-ups talked in whispers and we were left to imagine the very worst. But finally the day came when one by one all of us were to say goodbye to the school, to each other and saddest of all, to the Sisters. For me it was especially sad to say goodbye to my walking companion, Sister Elsie. And also to the two closest friends I had there. Another Elsie and her sister Nellie. I was never to see them again, and I wonder what happened to them. Have they ever wondered what happened to me? Many of my other classmates I would meet again, in another country. Mother didn't take us back to Rangoon; instead we went back to the hostel we stayed in during our holiday, and there awaited events. My brothers and I were together again!

CHAPTER NINE

War!

IN THE DECEMBER OF 1941, Japan declared war on Burma. To us girls at school it seemed like a dream. I am going back a bit in time from the last two paragraphs in the previous chapter just for a moment. We were now a part of a war that had been going on since 1939 and which had not touched us. We expected bombs to drop the very next day and we were more than a little scared and excited too – as one is at the unexpected. We collected in huddles round one another's beds that night after lights out. It was the first time Matron didn't come round with her lantern to see if we were all in bed. So we discussed the possibilities and the dangers that war would bring. It did not occur to anyone of us that Burma would be invaded. We did not know then that the enemy would end up on our doorstep, and that for some of us that would mean death or near-death.

I was only just eleven years old now, and once again life had taken another turn. I had not heard from my brothers and I had not seen my parents for some time. All my hopes and dreams seemed to be so far in the future that I was not sure that there would be a future. I who was usually so optimistic was now not so sure of anything. I was not afraid in one sense, because at that time and at that age I had not seen the true face of war. It was still something that had happened to others, so fear of war didn't enter into it. It was separation yet again from my brothers and the rest of the family that bothered me. Very selfish thinking! Later I would change my mind about things.

But nothing happened then, and the school closed for the

Christmas holidays. My parents came down and we went to the hostel for the short holiday. It was a joy to be with my brothers again, and I felt safe and secure. It was while we were there that Mother received a telegram from my eldest sister saying that the Universities were closing down till further notice and please to come and fetch them. Father decided that we would all go, as he wanted to make sure that his Mother, Grandma, was OK, and if need be take her and my Aunt and cousin out of Rangoon also.

Father used a Ford Vanette for the journey, knowing a car was not big enough for all of us on the return journey. He placed a mattress in the back and the three of us made ourselves comfortable there. We left Maymyo very early one morning, I think it was 17 December. The journey hit us with its old familiarity, reminding us of the journeys to Thandoung, and knowing that at one point we would be covering some of the route we used to take. Maymyo was further North of course so we had a greater distance to travel. It meant sleeping in a *dawk* bungalow. These were rest houses for travellers. There is usually a janitor in charge, but more often not. All a traveller needs do is drive in, chose a room and bed down for the night. It is usually a very bare place, sometimes there are beds, sometimes not, and one takes a holdall. I had one on my journey to school. Sleeping bags with pockets at either end, and flaps in the middle. Very handy things which roll up into a neat bundle. These *dawk* bungalows are mainly a roof over one's head. This first night we had a very unfortunate one. No electricity, no beds and the janitor had fled. We made ourselves as comfortable as possible, but it was to be a dreadful night. The heavens opened and there was a terrible storm. The windows rattled all night and didn't close properly so the rain came streaming in. We couldn't light the lantern because the wind kept blowing it out and we had nothing to eat because the spirit lamp would not work. We couldn't wait for the morning. It was a wild night, the thunder roared and the forked lightning lit up the room so that we had spots before our eyes. We had never been afraid of storms before but we were cold and tired, hungry and thirsty, and we could have done without one on this night.

Early the next morning, stiff and hungry, we piled into the Vanette and headed for the nearest Burmese village in search of food. What a relief to be full, satisfied and happy again. We continued on our way and that night stopped at another *dawk* bungalow, but so different to the last. Here was light, good beds – and best of all food. Burmese food is delicious with a taste that is like nothing on this earth! My brothers and I got out the cards and played happily, Tucker winning as usual, and then slept the sleep of the innocent. In other words – like logs! Next morning we were ready for anything. It was now 19 December and Father's birthday.

We arrived in Rangoon about midday and went straight to the college. It was deserted. We drove into the vast grounds expecting to see students around; instead there was a profound silence which was disturbing. Access into the place was easy, nothing seemed to be locked up and it was hard to imagine that people could leave a place like this; just walk out, in panic really. The place was dead, Rangoon seemed dead, for we had driven through silent streets; the tension in the air was unmistakable. It silenced us three and brought an unseen menace suddenly very close. But where were my sisters? We wandered around and finally found them. They had been left to themselves and had locked themselves in. Very relieved to see us, they brought their gear down and packed it into the back of the van and climbed in with Alan, Tucker and myself.

Next stop – Insein and Grandma's house. Here was a place we felt safe in, and although we had been away a while, it wasn't long before the three of us had dashed off to see our old haunts. The threat of war receded here in these much loved surroundings and we had the same feeling of freedom Insein always instilled in us. That night we did all the things we had always done. We played cards round our lamp-lit table, and the tucktoo heralded bedtime as always. The Horlicks came out and the 'squish, squish, squish' made our hearts glad. Bedtime was the same too. In the large four-poster – for the last time –

Alan flew his plane, Tucker drove his sports car, and I was the passenger ... All was the same! Yet it wasn't. The grown-ups had let us kids enjoy the last time they knew we would ever spend in the old family home, but in the morning everything had changed. Decisions had to be made – fast.

We went to Malagong to see Uncle Tom and for Father to have a long and serious talk with him. We had lunch there, with the finger bowls still in use, but it was a sad and silent lunch. Then the three of us set out to look at my own self's house and what was a last look at our childhood. All was lifeless. There were no Gurkha guards to stop us entering, nothing to stop us from wandering through the estate. The *godowns* were empty, the doors open for all to enter, no Burmese ladies chattering with their babies hanging in hammocks, no sound of happy laughter. Just silence. The tennis court was dirty and grass grew through the cracks; the machinery which once had seemed so menacing to us was now merely pathetic.

Then we went to the house. The door was open, the house unoccupied. We wandered through. Here was where my bed stood, here Alan and Tucker's, even to the scribbles on the wall which we had got into trouble over. Down in the dining room, and here was the spot where Tucker had slipped and sat on Twisty. There too was the window at which Father had sat during the riots with his gun in his lap. We went up and down, silently, each of us wrapped in our own memories. These stairs were the ones where I had taken my first adventure, barely eighteen months old and going down on my bottom. Walking down to the sheds where the trains had brought the paddy in – all silent and empty. Down by the river where we had watched the coolies loading the barges and going up and down the planks, never missing a step. Had there ever been life here? It was like a ghost town, yet this was where growing up began, and where our blissful days were spent, and where now, our childhood was coming to an end. We three knew this. Nothing would ever be the same. We were saying goodbye to a part of our lives we would never be able to go back to, never visit again for it might not even be here. Malagong had been ours.

Insein was Grandma's. Here was the very essence of who we three truly were, where we had moulded into a unit that was unbreakable, and which was never to break even though death would separate us physically in the future

Now this was over. The happy days of innocent childhood had to be left behind forever. Malagong was so many things to us; now we had nothing. It was as though we had betrayed the place by coming to say a final farewell, and leaving it to its fate. I wanted to say to the sad empty house, 'I didn't do this to you, for I love you too much, and I wouldn't leave you if the choice were mine.' But I said nothing, nor did my brothers. We went through the house silently for the last time and never once spoke to each other. Then suddenly the accusing rooms were too much for us, the memories too real and pressing and we went outside. The custard apple tree was still there, and the papaya tree. And there in one corner was the slab of stone with two names on it: 'Twisty' and 'Puck'. This was the last straw. We left and walked down the road where the boys had run over the *dhobi* and on which I used to walk in a huff, with my potty under my arm, to the main gate. Alan first, Tucker next and me, way behind. We never looked back, and we were never to see my own self's house again.

My parents asked no questions, and we made the journey back to Insein in silence, stopping on the way to see the school and the church. The school was closed but the church was still open. It is still open to this day and full too with worshippers. We couldn't bear to stay long. The lizard in the tower still lay across the lighted blue cross and like our tucktoo didn't need to move for his food came to him. We drove on, briefly passing the home in Shoay Dagon Pagoda Road, then past the Pagoda on the way to Insein.

That evening was the last we spent in Grandma's house. As we had bidden farewell to Malagong, so we said our goodbyes to Insein. We bathed with water from the kerosene cans heated underneath, and watched as it went through the floorboards and drained away. We had dinner and the lamps were lit. But this night we sat and looked over Grandma's garden and my green hill – over to the family well and the mango trees beyond. We had no heart for bolsters and when we went to bed, just curled up together close for comfort, and slept uneasily. Even the tucktoo said nothing! The next morning we left. The day was 21 December 1941.

As we were leaving Rangoon on the road to the North, a single plane flew overhead with Japanese markings. 'Reconnaissance,' my father said. None of us felt like conversation, just looked out through the back of the van knowing we were leaving all that we loved behind. By the time we reached Pyinama, Rangoon had its first bombing raid, and Father's boss and his wife were killed in that first raid.

We carried on, heavy at heart. Stopping only for food, we drove through the night. It was only when we reached Mandalay that Father stopped and we booked into the station hotel. There was unease everywhere and after Rangoon, Mandalay was the next biggest city. Father knew that would be the next bombing target. So we left early the next day, and finally back to the hostel in time for Christmas. Was it a good Christmas? I don't remember it too well. Father had to return to Lashio and we stayed on at the hostel and finally returned to school. Life had to continue. Food was still plentiful at that time and in Maymyo we did not feel the effects of the war, though Rangoon was now being bombed every day.

Then in the new year while we were sitting in the grounds of the school, an army man on a motorbike roared in and asked to see Sister Harriet. It was then that we received the news that the Army wanted to take over the school and all the girls had to be sent home. I have mentioned this before and all events are told as they happened in order from now on.

Mother and Father, because of the death of Father's boss, now left Lashio and came down to Maymyo. So we were all together. Singapore had fallen and things were getting very serious. Uncle Tom laid on a special train taking people out of Rangoon including the Governor General, and Grandma, my Aunt and cousin. Mr Walker decided to stay in Rangoon and sit out the war, which he did. He was an old man and the Japanese left him alone.

So they joined us in Maymyo also. Father had got us digging trenches, and it was hard work, but it occupied our minds and we were glad to be doing something. What were we waiting for? I was never clear about that at the time, but we had no school to go to and when would it ever open again anyway? We had not been bombed, though father was certain that Mandalay would be, and Maymyo was just above. So we waited for something to happen ...

Then one Sunday Father went to Mandalay with one of my sisters. It was a very quiet day, and after lunch we settled down for it was also very hot. The older ones had gone to their rooms for a rest, and we sat around wondering what to do with ourselves. Suddenly we heard the drone of planes and dashed out to investigate. The droning became louder, and finally we spotted the planes. Nine of them. By this time everyone else had left their rooms and joined us, and there we were, the whole lot of us, standing in the open with nothing between us and death. The hostel stood alone, with the railway station about four hundred yards to the front, and an army camp about a mile to the left of us, and mule lines behind that. And that was

King Mindoon Min's Tomb, Palace Grounds, Mandalay.

what they were after! It was quite fantastic, because we saw the
sun glinting on the hatches as the bomb doors opened, and it
was only then that realization hit us! Japs! We hit the floor of
the veranda as the first bomb fell, and then dashed indoors.
And there we stayed, all of us, heads down till the raid was
over. So much for the trenches we had dug. We felt very silly
and of course very stupid. But we had never heard the sound
of the Japanese planes and at that time could not identify them.
But we soon did! After they had gone, no siren warning, no 'all
clear' for it was so unexpected, we went out to investigate. The
bombs had dropped in a complete circle around us and it was
nothing short of a miracle that the hostel was still standing.

Father and my sister returned later to tell us that the nine
planes had also bombed Mandalay. Not a vast number of planes,
but it was just a beginning of what was to come.

That same day, my eldest sister joined the army as a nurse.
And not long afterwards the Japanese entered Rangoon, and so
began the march upwards, which was to devour the whole of
Burma.

CHAPTER TEN

Evacuation

T HE NEWS ON THE RADIO was not good, and we heard many rumours. We did not know if Uncle Tom had got out of Rangoon. All we did know was that he had got the Governor General and other important people out of Rangoon, laying on a special train which had also brought Grandma up to Maymyo, and then going on up North to take a flight out to India.

We also heard that they had let all the mental patients out of the lunatic asylum. I use that word because that is what they were called then. Also that the monkeys in the monkey village in the Rangoon zoo had been released. Apparently the big cats and the elephants and giraffes were still there. Father had a special interest in the giraffes for he had laid on the transport to take them to the zoo when they had first arrived in Rangoon. I remember that day.

Their keeper had come with them off the ship, and father had this huge open truck with deep sides into which they had been put. The route they were to take was up the Shoay Dagon Pagoda Road which had tramlines the length of it. It was then necessary to turn off right and into the end of the Sula Pagoda Road, then right into the road that led to the zoo. But of course there had to be a police escort, as the giraffe heads were higher than the tram electric cables. And of course the populace turned out in force. Everyone cheering for a very great many of them had never seen a giraffe before. It was quite a journey and my father was very relieved when he delivered them safely. Their keeper was quite a character and loved his charges. The male giraffe had a habit of picking him up by his belt when his back was turned with its front legs spread out. A very comical sight! I was never sure as a child whether this was a put-up job, between the giraffe and his keeper to keep the visitors amused, for we certainly were, and loved it …

A friend of ours was the son of the zoo keeper, and he used to help his father with the elephants. A baby elephant had been born and this lad had special charge over the little thing. It broke his heart to leave them behind, but there is a sequel to this story and if I don't tell it now, I'll never find reason to relate it later. The Japanese did look after the animals well, and after the war was over some years later, our friend returned to Rangoon and of course went to the zoo. Straight to the elephant house. And there were the elephants, and the baby too, but no longer a small elephant. He stood among the other people, when suddenly this elephant started to get agitated and came to the wall and reached out its trunk to where our friend was standing. And trumpeted, which gave everyone a shock. Not our pal. He jumped over the wall and to everyone's astonishment the elephant picked him up in its trunk. As he said later, and the onlookers agreed, that if it was possible for an elephant to cover someone with kisses, this one did. The reunion was complete, with the parents looking on and in their turn coming to welcome their old friend home. He was no longer a small lad now, but those elephants remembered him. He said the giraffes were there too and their keeper. We were very glad! But back to the story.

Food was getting scare now, because supplies were no longer getting through from the port of Rangoon. We used to use tinned milk anyway, Nestlé's condensed, I always loved it. As a child I would fill a saucer with two tablespoons of it and mix it with one teaspoon of cocoa powder. Try it! It is better than any chocolate you buy in the shops. Anyway we had plenty of tinned milk, bags of rice and lentils. *Dhal* we call it. And that was our daily diet, and even that had to be rationed for we did not know how long we would all be there. Sometimes we would have the odd vegetable, but that was rare. My *Ayah* remained in Rangoon, but our *chokra* Phythulli was with us. People were leaving the country rapidly, catching planes in the Northern Provinces of Burma. Others were walking out. The route they were taking was fairly easy, with *dawk* Bungalows on the way, and villagers to buy food from. Bridges were still intact then and some had bullock carts and other simple means of traffic. Cars were useless once the petrol ran out. Later some described this route as a long picnic. But this was before the Japanese cut the route. But while it was still clear Father decided we too would leave this way.

Mother started to get our clothes together. As we would have to carry our own things, we could only take essentials. Also some medical supplies like quinine for malaria and citronella oil to guard against insects. And of course iodine. Never go anywhere without iodine was Mother's motto! Father also arranged for us to be inoculated against just about everything. Every three days we had an injection of some sort or the other. Our arms were sore and we did not feel good at all. In fact at that time my brothers and I would wander about aimlessly, for we were not allowed to go far. And ask ourselves over and over the question mankind has never been able to answer in all honesty. Why must men and nations fight? Greed, power, envy? All those things and more. If neighbours cannot live in peace, but envy what others have and want it for themselves, then what hope has the world? At that age we talked of these things. Although Alan wanted to be a pilot and was eventually, and Tucker a racing driver, which he didn't become, and I an actress which I did – we still had other dreams that we wanted to fulfil together. We wanted to look after orphans. Alan if he couldn't be a pilot, he would opt for being a doctor and Tucker would do all the electrical gadgets for the home we would build for these children. He would have doors that opened automatically when you crossed a beam, he was going to have moving stairs going up and down – we would have cooking facilities that required food being turned out in a short time. In short my brother was inventing things in his mind that hadn't yet come about. I would be in charge of the household and for entertaining the kids, and others would work with us to be Mothers to the orphans. Those were our dreams, and we would happily plan all these things, still keeping our own individual hopes alive. Now all this looked like being a dead dream, a forlorn hope. Yet I do not think that our lives have gone by without wishing that we could have always been together to make those hopes and dreams and plan come true.

But Father was worried. His Mother, our Grandma was getting old. Could she stand that journey? The answer to be truthful was No. But we were all set to go with little choice, when Father came home with the news that the Douglas Dakotas that were bringing in the troops would take out evacuees. And priority would be given to the wives of Army officers. Grand-father had been in the British Colonial Army so we were eligible. But as it turned out, and we were grateful for this for no one should be singled out for favours – everyone who turned up at the army camp in Shwebo would be airlifted out. But there was a snag. We could only take out seventeen pounds of luggage each. Mother bought *pahs*. These are baskets made of soft matting, the lid being as deep as the base, so one covers the other. They are very light in weight.

With heavy hearts we packed our toys in a box and just left them. We gave our Hornby set away to a boy who was staying, his family were Burmese and would probably be allowed to remain in their home, but no one could be sure of that, and of course this wasn't always so, for many families went into concentration camps, which was what would have happened to us. Tucker took 'Woofles', his black toy dog, with him, Alan a little white dog which I have in my keeping to this day, and me my little teddy. Also a small 'wetums' doll which you could give a drink to, and it obligingly then in time wet its nappy. Nothing is new today, we had all those kind of things yesterday! My eldest sister was in the army, so my other sister was placed in charge of us three. Mother put 1,000 rupees in a money belt which my sister placed round her waist under her clothing. The rupee had better value in those days and that was that. My Aunt was in charge of Grandma and my cousin. Mother wisely put my sister – and no argument – in charge of us. Prudent move all round.

We had heard from Uncle Tom and he was safe. Still moving trains around in spite of the Japanese, though he was operating further to the north of Rangoon. Yet again he put a train at the disposal of refuges leaving Maymyo for Shewbo. The night we left was one I will never forget. As I mentioned before, the hostel was not far from the railway station so we walked along the track till we reached the station and the train standing there in the dark. A very dark night, and Grandma had to be helped all the way. No petrol, so no car and this was the shortest route. We carried our own *pahs*. My cousin's father, my Uncle had also joined us in Maymyo and he and my Father carried Grandma's and my Aunts' luggage. We walked along that track till dim lantern lights in the distance told us we were near the station. No electric lights at all, and it was well after midnight. The platform was crammed with people, all looking hopeless and tired, as we were. Some were sitting on their little bits of luggage, others seemed to have brought all their belongings with them. I do remember many arguments and raised voices for people were more important than luggage, and many stayed behind because they wouldn't part with their goods. We had the allotted allowance.

If there were many on the platform, there seemed to be as many also on the train. We did manage to find a small corner as others made room for us and we crowded in. Making Grandma comfortable, we three sat on our *pahs*. It was a third class compartment, in fact the whole train was third class – no comfort on this journey, getting people on board was more important. So all the seats were of hard slatted wood. We sat there for what seemed like hours till at last the train moved slowly out of the station. We could not see our parents in the darkness and we said our goodbyes silently. Grandma wept quietly in her corner. I had never seen my Grandma weep, she had always been the cornerstone of the family, and we realized that this could be the end of the unity we as a family had always been privileged to share. It was a sadness we could not cope with, and my brothers and I each remained silent with our own thoughts. I do know that mine were confused, miserable and I, who would always refuse to show my feelings and indeed my tears, was glad of the darkness. The only one who felt my tears and knew about them was my teddy. And he was only a toy! My cousin was near my Aunt, and my sister not too far from us. What they were thinking, I do not know. Their association with Burma went back so very many years, all that they had, all that they had built in those years was now gone. I have often been told here in England that over here people lost their homes and loved ones. I understand that. But their childhood is still in this country, the countryside is still here for them to walk through. We have only memories. We cannot go back to those places we knew so well, for the home in Insein has been obliterated from the face of the earth. After the war, Father located where the house once was because he found the well. The rest of the area for many square miles was totally flattened – no forest, no bamboo trees. No mango trees, no corrunder bush. Nothing! Total oblivion. My Father talked of it only once and never again. In our hearts we all knew that this was the end.

The night dragged through, and we slept fitfully against each other. It was very hot. We had taken a *chattie* of water with us, and we had to use it sparingly. It was for the seven of us, but others in the carriage had not brought water, so we shared with them. The water did not last long. We were to feel the need of water the next day, for we spent nearly a whole day in a siding outside Mandalay. Due to the extra bogies and the extra load, the train had to do the forty miles of steep gradients down the hill to Mandalay at a snail's pace. The result was a continual jerking motion through the night due to the constant application of the brakes. And when we did reach Mandalay it was to find that the line to Shwebo which lay north-east of Mandalay had been bombed. We could not proceed till it had been repaired. Uncle Tom to the rescue again. He was working desperately hard to keep lines up to the North open as long as he could.

EVACUATION

So here we were in a siding, in the blazing sun. No shade anywhere, no shelter within a mile of any Jap fighter who chose to strafe our train, had he been passing. I think many people were praying quietly.

So there we sat, huddled together. Miles of railway lines around us which reflected the sun, none of which was any use to our train. A train full of overcrowded, hungry and very thirsty people. Children crying, babies howling and for those little ones and the elderly a very hard time. We remained there till about 4.30 p. m. and then to everyone's relief we were once more on our way.

We had to cross the Ava bridge which spanned the great Irrawaddy River. It was a very long bridge and we crawled over. Later it would be bombed and no other trains ever went across. But we were fortunate. The other side the train stopped for refuelling and water, and a *burman* was selling oranges, which sold out in next to no time. We were also able to fill our *chattie* with water. All done through the kindness of the Burmese, for no one was allowed to leave the train. The train did have toilets, though it was quite an ordeal using them. One had to climb over other bodies, as they too had to climb over us. But at least they worked! We arrived in Shwebo at 8 p.m. that night.

Eyes heavy with sleep, stomachs empty and all but beyond food, and with tongues desperate for water, everyone piled out of the train, which had stopped yet again in a siding. So there was quite a drop to the ground. In the dark it was hard to see what was happening and the old people had to be helped. Quite a few fell. There were buses for the elderly and the very young, but the rest of the passengers had to walk. It was the blind leading the blind. I don't remember too much of that walk, I just followed my brothers who followed the ones in front of them who followed the ones in front of them etc, etc. I think I did that walk with my eyes shut! We arrived, and by this time it was very late. There was some food and something to drink, but everyone was too weary and miserable to think of anything but sleep. And this was on the floor in a vast room full of people. There were blankets and pallets to lie on, no beds. In silence we all lay down and sleep took over.

The next morning we three investigated our surroundings. We found that there were three double-storeyed buildings made of wood, the upstairs being one vast room which was where the soldiers billeted as a rule. One building was used as a reception and departure centre, the other two as sleeping accommodation for the evacuees with the downstairs being a dining area. Nothing fancy at all! Army style we all lined up with tin plates and the food was dished out. I don't really remember too much about how it tasted only that it seemed to be the same meal repeated over and over. But we were grateful for it anyway. Toilets and showers were in tin huts set apart from the main buildings, with only washbasins in the sleeping accommodation for basic use. The grounds of course were large, with the parade grounds and even a basketball court. We were to stay here for nearly a week, with the Japanese advancing ever nearer.

There were three flights each day, morning, afternoon and evening. The planes were B49s – Dakotas, as I said earlier. The runway consisted of three large fields put together. The planes brought in young soldiers who went straight to the front, and took evacuees out. The morning flight was calm, as was the evening, but the midday flight was rather turbulent. Something to do with the air flow over the Arakan Yomas which had to be crossed to get to Chittagong on the borders of India and Burma.

We awaited our turn. In vain! Then Grandma asserted herself and went to find out why. It seemed that people were being taken out in alphabetical order, and our surname was rather far down the scale. That was not the problem though. What Grandma discovered was that as more people arrived they were just added to the list, and when they arrived was not accounted for. So we were constantly being pushed down. In short, we would never get away, as many others would not either whose names came further down the alphabet. The A-Gs even if they had arrived the night before got on a plane. No one tumbled to this for three days, till Grandma made a fuss. So of course the order was changed and rightfully so. Though still in alphabetical order there were separate lists. The first to come were the first to go. We had to wait three days before our turn came, and in that time we made many friends. So many children, so we whiled away our time playing rounders – a version of baseball/basketball and we introduced the others to 'kick-the-can', our own special game.

I do not remember at that time being scared in the least, nor do I recall the other kids being too affected either. We were lulled into a sense of security because we were playing games, chatting and just being happy. Living for the moment. How easily one forgets the discomfort of yesterday, to enjoy the comfort of today. It was a false sense of security though, for the Japanese were only forty miles away when our turn came to fly out. There was still a shortage of food, but at least we did eat. If leaving Rangoon and Insein had affected us then, we were now caught up in the new things that were surrounding us now. Life was exciting for the moment. But only for the moment!

One thing did happen for me that was very personal and painful. As I said in another chapter, I had brought my doll and my teddy with me. My cousin also had a doll with her, which she didn't care about. This I did know! One night she decided to pass it on to another child. It was not an important issue with her, but it became something terrible for me. For my Aunt decided that my cousin was a generous and sweet child, and to all who would listen, implied that I was not. My tiny doll and my precious teddy came under attack and she suggested that I too gave them away. My teddy? The thought was awful, but my sister suggested that I gave my doll away. And this she felt I must do to preserve family honour: that is our family's honour, hers, Alan's, Tucker's and mine! So I got out my doll and gave her away. Teddy I held onto; he I would not part with under any circumstances. I will give credit to the others around us and especially Grandma who realized what was happening and stepped in and prevented my Aunt on insisting I part with Teddy also. It was a terrible time, and I lived with this terrible injustice for many years. What I didn't tell anyone was that I had the cotton flowered parasol I mentioned earlier, which my Mother had given me years before, which weighed next to nothing and was in my *pah*. I still have it. Safe! I had told no one, for I had just tucked it under the few things I was allowed to take. I never hated my Aunt or my cousin, but I didn't like them at that time, the pain they caused was so unnecessary.

The time had come. We sat with our bits and pieces around us and waited. The day dragged on, and we wondered if evening would ever come. Finally we got the call and went to the buses that were to take us to the 'airfield.' We arrived there about 5.15 p. m. in time to see the plane landing, and soldiers tumbling out with their kit and rifles. The looked so young and not much older than my sister. They looked lost and scared, and we felt very sorry for them. We knew the Japanese were moving fast and nothing was standing in their way and that our troops were being pushed back. It wasn't till we got to Calcutta that we discovered just how near they had been to Shwebo. If we had not got on that plane, two days later we would have remained in that army camp as prisoners of the Japanese Imperial Army. How many of these young soldiers would survive? We watched as they were lined up, called to attention, and then marched away. Our few days of security and just being children melted away as the horror of war and conflict once more touched us!

While we were waiting to board the plane, a Japanese fighter flew overhead, but did not attack. We had nowhere to go so just stood there silently and waited for whatever was coming. But thank God he flew away. The soldiers had marched off, and perhaps he did not see them, only a group of women and children. We climbed aboard. There were metal seats running down the sides of the plane, with indentations to denote each person's seat. Very much a troop carrier. Down the middle all the luggage had been placed and on these all we children sat. Each of us was given a bag in case of air sickness. When we were all settled, the engines were started. I'll never forget the feeling for it hit me quite suddenly, and judging by the faces around, most of the others were registering all kinds of emotions. There was no time to say, 'I hate flying', for the majority of us had never flown before, and we had no idea what it would be like. And we were leaving our homeland for who knows what lay ahead of us. We had no safety belts, and the grown-ups only had straps to hang onto, and we children were told to hang on to the legs of the grown-ups. Great! The take-off would be rough, the pilot said, so hang on. So we did and rough it was too. First the engines revved up, and we trundled forth. The pilot had to go to the very edge of the three fields, and when he got there suddenly the engines roared and with a burst the plane shot forward. A few people screamed as it bumped and jolted over the ground. It seemed an age before it left the ground. We could see trees whizzing past and we thought we would hit something, then with ears popping, we were up and away. Everyone had been holding their breath, it seems, for there was such a deep sigh from everyone. A deep sigh of relief.

It was a smooth flight with a few air pockets over the Arakan Yomas which caused the plane to suddenly drop making our stomachs heave into our mouths or so it seemed. Our pilot had warned us, so we were prepared and got used to them. Also he had us kids up into the cockpit in twos. What a wonderful sight it was. Burma below us in all its beauty and greenery, for it is a very beautiful country, full of rivers and green fields, teak forests, paddy fields and peace and beauty. Now being torn apart by guns and heavy artillery, with death everywhere. The world was not created for this – but greed exists, and the desire to subdue others exists, and even all of us, each in our own way, does this to our next door neighbour, or even our brothers and sisters. So war between countries is not unexpected.

Alan of course was in heaven up in the cockpit and asked the pilots question after question. What did this do, and what did that do and what happened when you did this, etc. He asked intelligent questions too, for they were happy to answer and show him. Other kids didn't get to the cockpit as they had their heads buried in their sick-bags, poor things!

An hour and a half later the lights of Chittagong came into view, and the plane began its slow descent. Once more we had to hang on to our elders, for we expected the landing to be as rough as the take-off. But it was lovely and smooth, for we were landing on a proper runway. We collected ourselves and our few belongings and trooped off the plane, glad to be in one piece.

Night had fallen, as it does quite suddenly in the East. We were taken to coaches which took us to an hotel for food – really great food this time – a wash and then we were off again. This time to a railway station and the 10 p. m. train which would take us to Howrah Station, Calcutta and our first real glimpse of India.

CHAPTER ELEVEN

India

WHAT MIXED EMOTIONS we had! Everything that was happening was like a dream sequence. All in slow motion! Our lives had been radically changed and what the future held we couldn't even guess at. Distances were far greater there than they are in England, so even at boarding school no child could pop home for the weekend. Once away from home, that was it for some months. When I had been sent to school I was separated from my brothers and that was a very lonely and miserable time. But now, we were sharing what was happening and that helped a great deal. Children are more optimistic than grown-ups for they do not see danger as adults do. Yet we were old enough now, eleven, twelve and thirteen years old – for there was a year between each of us – to realize that the possibility of never seeing our parents again was very real. Later we found out that our Father and Uncle Tom had come to the army camp at Shwebo to see us, only to find that we had left on the evening plane. We were never to see our precious Uncle Tom again, and Grandma never got over it. He was a man who was so greatly loved by one and all, and was such a very special person. One small thing I always remember about him, and maybe the rest of the family don't know this, but he loved the hymn, 'O God our help in ages past'. He and I often used to sing it together, just the two of us. And I knew it off by heart from a very early age. Even now when we wear our poppies and stand at cenotaphs all over the world and remember the dead of the two wars, and thank God for His deliverance, I find it hard to control the tears as they sing that age-old song. My

Uncle Tom! Our Uncle Tom! To everyone who knew him – the Mota Sahib!

We were now on a train, night again, on the long journey to Calcutta. The carriage we were in was a second class carriage with soft seats, so we were able to sleep. The night passed and then early in the morning we were transferred onto a boat and went up what I thought was a river, and which I realize now, looking at a map, was the inlet from the Bay of Bengal. A short cut across. I had never been on a ferry and this is what this was. I loved it! To be on a boat! I think I left my brothers behind as I explored and then stood for ages as I watched the water flowing past. It was a day's journey and as far as I was concerned could go on indefinitely. That later in my life I would spend a great deal of time on big white cruise ships was not a dream I had then, for in those days these kind of ships did not exist in the way they do today. Bliss! I just knew that something about that ferry spoke to me.

We left the ferry and transferred once more onto a train, for the last lap of the journey to Calcutta.

The trains in India and Burma were not corridor trains. Third class compartments were open with slatted bench seats, but with no door to the next bogie. Second and first class compartments had soft leather bunks, top and bottom, with their own bathroom. I use the word bathroom because that is how we always described the room where the toilet was. Still haven't got out of the habit! But it meant that food was brought to the compartment when the train stopped at certain stations, in tiffin carriers, and then removed at a later stage when the train stopped again. As evacuees we were being very well looked after. No one was being singled out for special treatment, for the whole train was second class. Since coming to India we had been more comfortable than we had been since leaving Maymyo. For Grandma's sake we were grateful for this, because she was so very weary, and there was such sorrow in her face.

She had come to Burma in the late 1890s when my Father was just one year old, and now nothing of her life was left. Her home, the one she had built was gone, all the things she loved had been left behind, and her sons! Would she ever see them again? We understood all this and tried to be quiet for her sake. But there was much to see on our journey. What amazed us though was the fact that the countryside here was nowhere as green as the Burmese countryside. How could this be? But that was a fact and we didn't dwell on it.

Calcutta at last! Howrah Station. Huge, noisy, people everywhere, and the odd cow walking around. We had come into it having crossed the Howrah Bridge. The Ganges flowing under it, very murky and brown. Where to now? I wish I could remember some things more clearly, such as who was giving the orders. I think it was army personnel for I vaguely remember some walking around. But we just followed where the others were going, and ended up in coaches yet again.

Fort William! A mighty fortress of the British Colonial Army! Huge colonnades and verandas and long rooms leading off them. Each family was accorded one of them, depending on the size of the family. We had two rooms. Then came the signing in, which had not happened before now. Each family had to give names, births etc. And who was who and what was what and who were the nearest and dearest who were not with us. We were very fortunate for the officer taking the roll call recognized our name and asked us if we were related to my Father, whom he named. We were indeed his children, my sister informed him, and yes this was his Mother and sister, and he said, 'Anything you want, just ask, I know your Dad well!' As my sister said later, in Burma he was known, as Grandma and Uncle Tom were, but we did not expect it when we reached India. The world is a small place!

We stayed in Fort William about three weeks or so. There was no news of our loved ones left behind, except for the fact that the Japanese had moved further up. They had taken Mandalay and Shwebo two days after we had left the camp. Those who were still there were now prisoners of war. Grandma lived from day to day, praying and hoping. We three took a trip into the main centre of Calcutta to buy a few clothes for we had very few. We were to know Calcutta well some years later, but for now we were confined to the Fort to await new instructions. These soon came.

There were several places that evacuees were being sent to, and our destination for the time being would be Dehra Dun, even further North, at the foothills of the Himalayas. Added to which we had an Aunt and Uncle who lived there.

We were sorry to leave Fort William, as we had made even more friends there, but we were in others' hands and had little choice. The usual mode of transport turned up, and we all piled in; a convoy of coaches, which took us to Howrah Station. The journey to Dehra Dun was to last three days and we were very grateful that once more we would be travelling in some comfort. None of these journeys had cost any of the evacuees any money, for many had come out with nothing, and my sister had to keep what she had for the time when the army no longer felt responsible for us.

It was very hot, and there was little wind, so we all suffered in many ways. Babies and the elderly fared the worst. All the windows in the carriages were fitted with mosquito netting screens, alongside the glass windows you could pull up and push down. But there were also wooden shutters, and we were soon to find out why. We went through a part of the country which looked like desert, and we had a dust storm. Don't ask me where it is on the map, I just don't remember. But it was terrible. In spite of the shutters, and the glass, the dust got in. I call it dust, because it wasn't sand like the Sahara, and it was most strange. It seemed to come through every tiny crevice and hole and got into our clothes, our lungs, our hair – the lot. It seemed hours before we were out of it. Thankfully the train stopped soon after and gave everyone a chance to get out and try to clear the compartments of dust. Also to have a drink and food, which was very welcome. But we were all very weary, and seemed to have travelled for weeks with no end in sight. Would we ever have a home again? No one could answer that question.

Arriving in Dehra Dun, once more on coaches, we were taken to another Army camp. This time it was spread out over a large area. Unlike Fort William in Calcutta, we had to share large dormitories, and this was not so good. But at least we had beds to sleep on, and the grounds looked promising to us children. Plenty to occupy our imaginations, and we made good use of the time there. We were taken to meet our Aunt and Uncle and they were to prove very good to all of us. Many years later we were going to be able to repay that debt ...

How many weeks were we there? Probably five or more, and then came another move. This time, 4,000 feet up into the Himalayas to a place called Mussooree. We went in buses which carried other local passengers, which meant we had chickens as companions also, and people hanging on everywhere and sitting on the roof of the bus as well. It was a journey never to be forgotten – ever! The whole way up was a series of hairpin bends and we had a *kamikaze* driver determined to send us all hurtling into eternity. He careered round those bends without a care in the world, while the passengers on the roof hung on for dear life, and those hanging onto the outside handles seemed to fly round those corners with their legs in space. Yet no one screamed, no one told him to slow down. I can only suppose this was normal for most of them and they had got used to it. Certainly familiarity breeds contempt so they say, and time too must have given them some sort of trust in the driver, for when we finally arrived in Mussooree they all waved cheerfully to him, assuring him they would see him soon. I hoped we never would!

We were taken to a place overlooking the mountain range, and it was very beautiful. The air was crisp and clean and we were accommodated in a large building which was obviously a colonial establishment of some kind, for it was very imposing, with large verandas and terraces. We even had a 'flat' of our own. This was to be the end of the line, where families would have to make decisions and then go their own way. But there was help. For all the families were given money to buy kitchen equipment and other necessities. So we could cook for ourselves now and live independently of others. My sister started to look around for schools for us. She would use some of the money Mother had placed round her waist in the money belt, and then she would return to Dehra Dun and join the army as a nurse. Grandma and my Aunt would go with her, as our Aunt and Uncle had offered them a place in their home. My cousin would come with me to the boarding school that had accepted us.

My brothers and I were to be separated yet again. Their school was over eight miles from ours, and the only way to see each other would be to walk those miles. So it would be some time before we were together again.

CHAPTER TWELVE

The Himalayas

THIS CAN'T BE TRUE! This I kept telling myself. We were in
Mussooree in the Himalayas, and all around us was the most
beautiful scenery in the world. We had left home, family, all
our childhood behind, and the only thing I had to hold onto
was the reassuring presence of my brothers. And now I was to
lose that again.

The school my cousin and I were to go to was, as I said,
eight miles out of the town. The only way to get to it was by
tonga, or by walking. *Tonga*! How do I explain them? These

The Himalayas.

were like a rickshaw, only more sturdy, with a bar in front and a bar at the back. Two men stood inside the bar in front and pushed, and two men stood at the back and pushed. That is if you were going uphill. If you were going downhill the order was reversed, for then they had to act as a brake instead. The roads were very steep, and made of sand and stone. Every three yards there was a concrete ridge about six inches high laid across the road. This was to act as a brake going down the steep roads. It was very strange! The *tonga* would go down at an angle from ridge to ridge, left to right, then bump over the ridge and then go from right to left. Going up was a strain on the men, so passengers (except for the hard-hearted) got out and walked. There were also conveyances that two men carried, rather like a black cigar. I never ever sat in one. My cousin did, for at one point in our stay up there, our former pastor from Rangoon paid Mussooree a visit and arranged for us to be fetched by one of these things to spend the day with them. They only carried one and we were supposed to take it in turns for we had ten miles to go. But my cousin took the first turn and then refused to get out, so I had to walk the ten miles there and back. I was always told, 'She is smaller than you, so she must be given preference.' Smaller was only by about six months! Very unfair! But back to the school.

It was in a beautiful place. Set into the side of the mountain, with views stretching to the far horizon. We could see the lights of Dehra Dun at night and in the far distance the hazy lights of Saharanpur. And very often there would be mist which crept up the mountainside and enveloped us. But we would watch it unravel, like a huge roll of cotton wool, slowly unwinding across the plain and then up the mountain till it reached us. A marvellous sight to behold. For playing fields we had what we called flats. These were large sections of ground hewed out of the mountainside and concreted with high wall and wire fencing. There was the top flat for daytime breaks, and the bottom flat for games. But this we had to reach by over a hundred steps. Ah well!

The school itself was comfortable enough, with large windows and lovely views, and the dormitories were OK, with one mammoth problem. The bathrooms were outside, with the toilets and showers there. All we had in the dormitories were washbasins. To reach the bathrooms there was a covered walk, fenced in because of bears which turned up every so often, and monkeys. It was a brave child who went there after dark, but it would be a miserable night at times if one didn't. So often we would wake one of the others up to accompany us, only to find that a whole lot of kids would have been lying there in the dark trying to find the courage to ask another. Very soon we all came to an agreement. No one was to suffer if they needed to get up at night. One for all and all for one! It was always scary none the less, because bears did appear at times and we always expected to see one. The Matron had a room off the dormitory, but she slept like a log and didn't like to be woken up and it wasn't to our advantage to wake her, for we would never have heard the end of it.

Then there was the problem of church. This school was also Church of England, and so we had to go to church each Sunday. As this was in the town we had the eight-mile walk there and back. We started at 7.30 in the morning to get there for the 10.30 a.m. service, which lasted an hour. Then we had the walk back, all uphill and we would get back to the school about 3.30 to 4 p.m., very tired and very hungry for we would not have had even a drink of water. Food on a Sunday was a loaf of bread with the insides removed, and then added to mince and onions and then put back into the hollow loaf. And baked! Hard to believe, but that is what we had. Actually it tasted quite good in its own way. I didn't mind the walk each Sunday because I was able to go into myself and hope and dream and imagine all kinds of things. The views were lovely too, and though we were so uncertain about everything, I still couldn't help being lifted up by the mountains. Only on two occasions were we to see the top of Mount Everest, and that was very rare for we were quite a distance away, but there was a park and gardens we were sometimes taken to – another long walk – and an old Indian worked there. He told us that yes, it was Mount Everest, but it only appeared when there was low cloud enveloping the mountains and then the peak of Everest would stand out. And so it was, though I still find it hard to believe. It was from this park that we could see the mountain fortress where the Dalai Lama was staying after having to leave Tibet. In the park some Italian prisoners of war also worked. They were very happy, and as far as I know, didn't want to escape. They were glad to be out of the war.

Church was the same as at St Michael's in Maymyo. Having to kneel all the time, and feeling tired and bored and usually very thirsty. So Sunday was not exactly a day of rest. We didn't have much free time at this school, for we even had lessons on a Saturday morning. My cousin and I were not doing too well at our lessons. We had arrived in the middle of a term, and we were so anxious and unhappy for a lot of the time that it was hard to concentrate. Especially hard was Urdu class. We had learnt Burmese in Rangoon, and spoke some Hindustani as we all did. But Urdu? Read from right to left and me being three years behind the others? No way! And the Urdu Master realized this, so I was excused from the class. This meant I could wander at will, making sure no one saw where I went. I would go to the bottom flat, and creep through a hole in the wire netting, and scramble around the mountainside. A dangerous thing, I can see that now, but it meant freedom to me.

In spite of the odd good moments, things were far from easy for the two of us. This was a school of children with very wealthy parents, and we were mere evacuees taken in by kind permission of someone or the other. We didn't have the kind of clothes the others had, and in fact our wardrobes were very sparse. So we were bullied. But not for long. I was brought up to despise bullying in any form, and when it came to being bullied, and especially my cousin, then the bullies more than met their match. I wasn't brought up with boys for nothing. Word soon got around to leave us alone, but even more so when other kids who had been bullied joined us. I did not like getting a reputation for being a tough kid, but we were stuck in a place far from our family with no one to defend us.

There was one teacher there who for some reason decided to target us. One day, I was talking to friends and twirling a small key I had on a string on my first finger. It flew off and unhappily landed on the shoulder of this teacher as she passed by. It was very light and did not harm her and I said sorry. But she turned round and slapped my left cheek with her right hand, and then with the back of her hand she slapped my right cheek cutting it open with the rings she wore. I then did something I never thought I was capable of doing. I leapt at her and got my hands round her throat and shook her. I was half her size, but I held on, blood streaming down my face and my friends had to drag me off. A combination of the treatment we were having, the not knowing if we were orphans or not, the separation from all those we loved, and the total injustice of the moment was too much. But it was a moment of awareness for the teacher herself for she knew she had done something wrong. She took me to have the cuts dressed and from that day on we were friends. She loved gardening and would ask me to help her. I think she had her own problems and inadvertently taken it out on me. I was very sorry that I had done what I did, and would never again lose my cool as I did then. But it turned out well ... I'm not sure I deserved that, but heartache reaches a certain point in all of us and I was still a child.

Then our English teacher decided to do a musical play. I was chosen to play Dora the Dunce! But in the play she turns out not to be a dunce at all. I didn't care what I played. I was going to be on stage again and that was good. It is always a home-coming for me when I step onto a stage. There are times when I stand in the wings saying to myself – what am I doing here, I must be mad, and what is my first line, and feeling my mouth dry and knees weak and then going on stage and feeling at home. This is where I truly belong. Perhaps it is where Gracie – the Grace that is – can hide her true identity! So we rehearsed and the time came to do the play. I'll give you just one guess where! Yes, in the town, and an eight-mile walk. But that was a moment of joy for me!

My brothers came to see us just once in all this time. What

a reunion and what a time of sharing together. I had so missed them. They were fortunate for their school was near the town, and being boys they were allowed out of the school at weekends. We had no such luck. We were taken for walks at the teacher's whim, so it was not very often. But when we did it was lovely. Lily of the valley grew in abundance, and what we called Bible fern. This was a very delicate lacy fern, and I took a sprig and placed it in my Bible. I still have that Bible, battered and worn through the years, so I have put it away safely.

These things were just passing moments in a barren place. No one had come up from Dehra Dun to visit, even though my cousin's father had now arrived there safely. My sister was working hard, and was now posted to a place near Bombay. Then I had a letter saying my Mother had come out of Burma. She was able to get the last flight out of a place called Myithina in the North, and was now living with another cousin – the one whose wedding I wasn't allowed to be a bridesmaid at if you remember. My sister was with her. I could hardly contain my excitement, for now I could go home. Home was wherever Mother was. But it was not to be. She decided that we would remain in our boarding schools till the Christmas holidays. That was a very hard blow to take.

The cold weather started to settle in, and my cousin and I didn't have enough warm clothes, and the Matron did nothing about it. I caught bronchitis very badly. No doctor was called and my condition grew worse. I was losing weight and coughing very badly and had a constant temperature. Other girls were sharing their warm clothes with us, but being prone to chronic bronchitis I was a ready-made target to get ill. No Po-Ho to rub on my chest as Mother used to do. I would have welcomed it. We wanted the school to contact our family, but they refused. Letters we wrote home were always read, and if we wrote anything that was considered wrong, we were made to rewrite the letter. So we did the only thing we knew. We refused to write at all, and in spite of my weakness I held out for the both of us. I knew that I would die if nothing was done. It worked! My cousin's father came to the school – in a *tonga* and unannounced, so everyone was caught in the act so to speak. He took one look at me, and removed us from the school there and then. What he said to the headmistress I never knew, and what Grandma did about it later on, I do not know either, but I do not think it was left unfinished. As for me, I was put in the *tonga* and stayed in it the whole way, wrapped up. The jolting and the bumps didn't matter. I felt terrible, but I knew that at last I was safe. Even the journey in the bus down the mountain to Dehra Dun didn't worry me. Grandma took charge. She was a nurse and she put me to bed and got a doctor. It was eighteen months before I was really fit for anything, so bad was I this time.

Then Grandma had a letter from Mother saying they had no right to take me from the school, and that I was to be taken back straight away. Grandma refused, and so began a tussle between them. Mother's argument was that I was always a little stoic and probably not as ill as I made out. I never complained, I never cried, I didn't like to show my pain, so Mother assumed that it was because it was never that bad. But this time I didn't have the strength to do anything. I was skin and bone and very lucky to be alive. I was saved from what I considered certain death if I was returned to that school, by the news that Father had come through.

The Burma trek it was called. Not the cosy one we were originally intending to go on, but a trek through jungle, and marshes, and bogs and rivers in flood. Snakes, scorpions and other animals. Dysentery, malaria, and everything one could think of, was what thousands faced trying to escape the Japanese. Thousands just walked west towards the India border, and many hundreds and hundreds would never make it. My precious Uncle Tom was one. We do not even know if he has a grave. People fell and others were too weak to bury them. Our little dog Mary was with Father, and he had to shoot her because she was suffering so badly. My Father himself had a poisoned leg, and he put leeches on it, and they sucked out the bad blood and pus, and saved his life. Many friends who started that trek we never heard of again. Only two in a family of fourteen we knew, came out alive. No one has ever made a film of that trek, and I don't think anyone could. It was a walk from evil to freedom and all those who died were mourned, and those who made it were glad that they had. Mother went to Calcutta to wait, and finally Dad's name was on the board of survivors and she went to the camp where he was. Planes couldn't drop food, for the jungle was too dense and no one had the strength to climb those vast trees. And it wasn't till the first stragglers came through and staggered into the first village that the army and Red Cross knew what was happening. First astonishment and then horror as the ragged, sick and desperate people filtered through. Then things began to move and teams went in as far as they could, to help. It was to be a sad and long task, for even then many died. My Father survived. Mother hardly recognized him, but for his hat which he still wore. It was burnt round the edges for someone had thrown it into a fire, and he had rescued it. But he was a very sick man, and it would be a long time before he would be fit again. But even then, never fully fit.

CHAPTER THIRTEEN

Reunion

WE WERE STILL IN DEHRA DUN when word came through about Father. And the news had to be broken to Grandma about Uncle Tom. Father had met some of the people who had been with him, so he knew that our dear and loving Uncle had died from exhaustion. He was a very heavy man, and it was too much for him.

My dear sweet Grandma, who had already lost most of her past, was now to know she had lost one of her sons. Of course, she took it as we knew she would – with great dignity. But she was never to fully recover from that loss, and there was always a sadness and frailty about her from then on. She never ceased to give us her support and love, but so often we would find her sitting quietly in her rocking chair, with her hands folded on her lap and gazing into a space filled with whatever only she could see. When her time came to go, well into her eighties, she went as quietly and serenely as her own life had been. She just lay down, went to sleep and never woke up. So many years have gone by, but for me my Grandma lives on in my heart, and is part of the hopes and dreams that only she knew about, so many of which she would have been so pleased to have seen come to pass. Not all of them, for I have had many setbacks many disappointments, many deliberate hurts come my way, yet the hope she gave me, will never die. She knew the sorrow that so many had to face in the war, she was not alone in that. Many lost many sons and fathers and husbands and she ached for them all, and she never blamed God, she never said, 'Why?' to Him. She knew what the world of greed, envy and the need for power, did. Man has a choice, he has free will and the consequences for the world in general affect us all in one way or another. I miss my Grandma.

There was no more talk about returning me to that school. Father said no. He knew his Mother would never, and had never interfered in his marriage, unless she had very good reason, and in this instance he trusted her judgement for she had seen my condition and Mother had not.

So the day came when we boarded the train for Bombay. My brothers were still at their school, and they were happy there. They were to come home for the Christmas holidays. The year was 1942.

I was still ill and coughing and had not put on much weight, though I was stronger. So I spent the journey curled up in a corner, and slept a great deal. It was hard saying good-bye to my Aunt and Uncle for they had been very kind to us. They kept buffaloes and their milk is wonderful. My Aunt used to make curds out of the milk and I loved this. She said it would build me up, and I am certain it did. She also had a piano. One of the long oblong ones which are very rare and precious, and I got my first real longing to learn to play as I tinkled on that piano. I do play today, but am no concert pianist, just someone who likes to sit at the piano and sometimes play as friends and family join in. And in worship services too. Nothing special!

Arrival in Bombay, and Mother's face when she saw me. She was appalled and kept saying, 'Oh, my baby!' I didn't mind that one little bit. My Father just picked me up and held me as he had so often in the past when I had been hurt in some way. I felt safe again.

My parents had rented a flat in a part of Bombay called Colaber. The sea was very close, and we were on the third floor. We looked over an Indian Army parade ground, and I used to watch each day as the lads went through their drill. They got used to seeing me and in a strange way without words being spoken we got to know each other. At the end of their parade time when they were dismissed I would get smiles and waves from them. I tried not to miss a day. We also discovered other friends who had settled in Bombay. Victor's parents for one, though Victor was at school as were my brothers, and Freddie's parents. We seem destined to follow each other around. But one of our other friends lived close by, and early each morning took her baby son for a walk on the sea front. So I used to join her every day. The sea air was doing me good, and with good food, and the fact that I was with my parents again I was happier and better then I had been for some time.

We often watched the fishermen bring in their catch, and one day they brought in a shark. I had never seen one in real life, and the way it snapped at one and all, with its small eyes glittering, was an experience. Though I must admit, if I had been caught in a net, I too would be snapping and angry. I don't know what they did with it, I didn't ask!

We made excursions to the centre of the city, going by tram, sometimes in a *garry*. That is a closed carriage rather like the old stagecoaches, with window shutters one could pull down. I remember there was Flori-bunder and Bori-bunder round which the traffic would flow, and of course Victoria Station where we had arrived which was a terminal. Bombay is an isthmus – water on three sides, and it is reached by a long causeway. In those days it was a beautiful city with large blocks of flats overlooking the sea, and it must be so today. I have not been back. But even then there were so many poor. The beggars were everywhere, as in Burma, and many were lepers. There is a class system there which seems immoveable, and so sad. Men are not equal there, but this is so everywhere. My father was a man, like his brother Uncle Tom, to whom all men are equal. He treated all men with respect, and as a result they respected him. When my father died, there was no room in the church for the people or the flowers. Even the bus driver and the conductor from the bus he used to travel on each day came to pay their respects. People we didn't know came – but he knew them. He had talked to all who came his way, and made friends all over the place. They came from North, South, East and West, and it was a very humbling experience. I wish this was so for all of us. That we too could accept all people as they are without looking at their clothes, or their homes, or the money they have – and feel superior in the way that we all do at times and should not!

Another place was Malaba Hill. This was where the Pharsee Tower of Silence was. It was a burial place really and hard to talk about so I won't. But it was a beautiful part of Bombay and where there is a famous beach and holiday centre. We never went there. But we did go to a place called Jehu. This was outside Bombay and a stretch of lovely white sand and coconut trees. We would spend time there, swimming and splashing around and jumping the waves. I had never seen the sea before we came to Bombay and this was a revelation to me. It was wonderful! There seemed no end to it, it seemed to stretch out to eternity, and I wanted to see where that was. One day I would sail the oceans, but I didn't know this then. For now, it was just a wonder to me. And I was getting stronger, though still coughing.

Time passed, and then the moment arrived when my brothers would be home with us. The flat we were in was to be taken over again by its owners, so we moved to the manse with our Pastor from Rangoon and his Family. It was a huge place, so there was room for us. My father had joined the RAF and was up in Rawalpindi. It was India then but Pakistan now. So we only saw him from time to time. We were still very poor, but Father was working again so it seemed that gradually we would be able to get a home of our own. But this was not to be, for as you will see, no sooner had we all been reunited, then we were to separate yet again.

My brothers were home. What joy there was to be together with them once more. My Grandma, Uncle, cousin and Aunt had their own flat, so it was just us three and Mother with the Pastor and his family. Christmas was very near, and we knew there would be no money for presents. But there was a Christmas tree, and there would be a carol service. No going out in an open lorry as we had in Burma. I was still not allowed out in the evenings when the air was a bit fresh, so I would have missed out anyway had they done so.

Christmas morning arrived. Underneath the tree were piles of presents, and we thought maybe there was something for us. But we watched as the Pastor's children opened present after present from America, from the congregation, from their parents, and there was nothing for us at all. We knew my parents were barely surviving, we understood that, and we had to pay for our board and lodging, but to sit and watch the delight on other children's faces when we didn't even have a crumb, just about broke our hearts. We could not understand why there was nothing from anyone. We three felt sick to our stomachs. The reality was that no one even considered how it was for us. We had no money, we were poor and what could be done? Nothing. And nothing was done. Yes, we had a Christmas dinner, but we had no toys to play with. Tucker had Woofles, Alan his dog and I my teddy. They were a great comfort. Our Pastor had been able to get out of Burma with all their things, so they lost nothing. I don't think, truthfully speaking, for they were lovely people, that it occurred to them how three young children would feel. Yet we smiled and for Mother's sake made the best of things. It was not easy for her at all. Other people like us were in the same situation. Victor's family had also got out early and his father's firm had moved them lock stock and barrel to India so they were all right as well. My Father's boss had been killed in the first air raid, and with him all Father's hopes. But that is the way things go in life and we still had each other, which was the main thing. But I have to be honest. I felt terrible on that day. God suddenly seemed to have disappeared and my guardian angel seemed no longer by my side.

I felt a sense of injustice and shame, and bewilderment that day, and it taught me a lesson I have never forgotten. Never turn away someone in need, never withhold from someone who has not when it is in your power to share. I am not a paragon of virtue, not at all. I have many faults, but some of the lessons I had to learn the hard way has enabled me to make sure I do not treat others in the same way.

Christmas passed, and it was time to return to school. But what school? There was no going back for me to the Himalayas, and what was to happen to Alan and Tucker? We hoped that we could settle in Bombay and go as day pupils. But it was not to be. Father was to be sent to Calcutta and Mother was going to join him. We were to be sent to boarding school, yet again. Was I going to be separated from my brothers once more and never see them for months?

No. For we were all to go to a brother and sister school in the South of India in a place called Bangalore. We had met up with Victor and Freddie, who were not coming with us. Victor I think went to a place somewhere in the hills, Freddie stayed in Bombay. So it was goodbye time again to our parents, and by now Father had earned enough money for us to be fitted out with school clothes, and the other odds and ends needed. This was another new place, another new school, another adventure! Or would it turn out badly?

It was now 1943. I was twelve years old, feeling I had lived a lifetime. I was being given something called Angiers Emulsion which was doing me some good. I was also being given raw eggs whipped in milk, and as yet the doctors hadn't given me permission to run around like other kids for I was still coughing. I put up with this for the first few months then decided enough was enough. Strength had returned to my limbs and I began to train. I started to run, then was put in the basketball team, and I never looked back. I ended up a good athlete and an asset to the school, but, that was not what I wanted to be! But to boarding school we went, and the day came when we three were taken to Victoria Station and boarded the train for the two days and one night it would take for us to reach Bangalore.

I have always loved train journeys and this was no exception. We were in a second class compartment and comfortable. Our food was brought to us at various stops and because we knew the two schools would be close together, and that my brothers would be able to visit each Saturday, we were happy. It also turned out that we attended the same church. Methodist this time as the schools were.

We arrived and went to our new schools. What we saw reassured us, and when I walked into my class for the first time, a whole group of kids stood up and yelled 'Gracie'. We were boarders, but it seemed as though all my friends from Maymyo and from Rangoon had settled in Bangalore, and we were together again. Sadly some were missing never to be heard from again, but this was like home from home, and as it proved to be, a new beginning for my brothers and I. We were to remain in Bangalore for the next three years, never going home. My Mother came to us at Christmas and we stayed in the school, but with total freedom. The summer holidays were the same, except for one summer which we spent on a farm. I was with the two girls from that family in my school, and my brothers with their three brothers in theirs. Their Mother had a farm outside Bangalore and it was arranged for us to go there. It is a story in itself – maybe to be told at a later date, for so much happened there, so many unexpected things, like a panther falling down a dry well, and a plane crashing, and one of the dogs being killed by a cobra which we then had to kill with our catapults … so much. But not here, not now. That is another story. But in that school friendships were cemented which remain to this day, characters were moulded and formed, and for myself the beginnings and stirring within me that one day I might – just might – realize some of the hopes and dreams I had as a very small child.

A Child in Burma

This brings me to the end of this first chapter of my life. Burma to India. But in the next three years, the small child became a teenager ... and life continued.